MW01659656

Maintain A Keeper

A Woman's Guide to Loving & Understanding Her Man

To! Tricia
May God carry you on
his wings & Guide you
Thank
Love
[illegible]

Maintain A Keeper

A Woman's Guide to Loving & Understanding Her Man

Tracee Stukes

Chocolate ICE LLC
Chocolate Ice Publishing

MAINTAIN A KEEPER * A WOMAN'S GUIDE TO LOVING AND UNDERSTANDING HER MAN.

Copyright © 2006 by Tracee Stukes. All rights reserved. Printed in the United States of America. No part of this book shall be reproduced or transmitted in any form or by any means, electronic, mechanical, magnetic, photographic including photocopying, recording or by any information storage and retrieval system, without prior written permission of the author or publisher except in the case of brief quotations embodied in critical articles or reviews.

Written by Tracee Stukes (except where noted)
Cover design by Juan L. Ortiz – Chocolate Ice Publishing
Edited by Ernestine Stukes & Larry Ingram – Chocolate Ice Publishing
Typesetting & interior book design by Ernestine Stukes – Chocolate Ice Publishing

ISBN #0-9777769-0-5
Library of Congress Control Number: 2006921721

Stukes, Tracee
*Maintain a Keeper * A Woman's Guide to Loving & Understanding Her Man*
Published by:

Chocolate ICE LLC
Chocolate Ice Publishing
2065 Fulton Street, Suite #1
Brooklyn, NY 11233
(347) 432-5456
Toll Free (877) Stukes1
Email: chocolateice..publishing@yahoo.com
www.chocolate-ice-publishing.com
www.myspace.com/chocolate-ice-publishing
Visit our weblog of expressions @ www.chocolateice.blogmaker.com, http://chocolateice-publishing.blogspot.com

To purchase a copy of Maintain A Keeper or any other Chocolate Ice Publishing titles go to www.chocolate-ice-publishing.com, www.amazon.com, www.barnes&noble.com, www.booksense.com or you can call the above number or write to the above address.

Printed in the United States of America

Testimonials

Lisa Wilson – Writer, Mother, Wife, San Diego, CA

This guide is wonderful and informative and I also enjoyed all the inspirational poems throughout the book.

Tom Anderson, Corporate Attorney

Tracee your guide says everything I have been trying to express to my wife for years. I gave my wife the guide and now our relationship is better for it. The lines of communication are wide open. It's wonderful. Thank you.

Tyesha Kee – Newlywed

When I read this book, I shared it with my then fiancé before we got married and we discussed all the issues in this guide and oh my God, I have discovered so much more about my fiancé who is now my husband. Our relationship is dynamite. This is a must guide for anyone who is about to get married.

Inez Rutling, Brooklyn, NY

I have read so many books on this subject that I began to give up until I read your guide it was very informative and enlightening. I was impressed.

Tanya Wilson, Richmond, VA

This guide was given to me as a gift from my spouse and I was like what is this for I think I understand you well enough, well when I finally did read your guide my eyes where open and I really didn't understand my spouse and I had to apologize to him. Thank you so much. Our relationship was on the rocks and I can honestly say your guide has help to save my relationship. With men they do speak a different language. My spouse was reaching out to me by giving me this book, I am glad he reached out and I read your guide.

Nyita Roberts, Atlanta, GA

Poems you have through the book are very spiritual and uplifting. You are a God send. Thank you and God Bless.

Lisa Jones, Baltimore, MD

Very, very, very easy read. Straight to the point. Men are not from Mars. They are just men. I just love your guide. I could go on and on but I don't wan to take up of anymore of your time. When is the sequel coming out?

Myria Lopez, Philadelphia, PA

Tell all the men who shared their wisdom and feelings with you, Thank you. On behalf of all the women around the globe thank you gentlemen, for being honest and open in sharing.

Interview with Michelle, NYC

How do you like the guide? I love it, I love it, I love it! Will you recommend Maintain A Keeper to your friends? Heck yeah! They can't read or touch my book, they have to get their own, so I will be ordering more. Thank you so very much Tracee. All I can say is that I love it, I love it, love it! I can't wait to have you come and speak at one of our seminars. You are welcome and thank you for purchasing my book and spreading the word. I'm always available to my readers. It's the readers like you that have inspired me to do what I do.

Timonthy Knight – Hackensack, NJ

Every woman in the United States, better yet in the world should own this book. Me and the fellas was just saying we are tired of all the men bashing. When is someone really going to write a book, movie or any darn thing that uplifts us and shows that there are some really damn good men out there. We are not all dogs. Maintain A Keeper hit it right on the head. If you don't already have this book go and get it right away. Fellas buy the book for your woman if you have too. Yes, yes, yes and you are woman who wrote this guide I am amazed. Where were you when I got married two years ago? Thank you, thank you and God bless and good luck. If you are writing the sequel feel free to email me.

To submit your testimonial please send to:

testimonial@chocolate-ice-publishing.com

When you read this guide have an open-mind!

It's been a long year in creating this guide. I felt it in my spirit that this guide had to be written. Our men are struggling to stay with the women they love and the women just don't see it and when they do finally see it, it's too late. My guide is plain and simple, like they say K.I.S.S. – Keep It Simple Stupid. I'm not a doctor, psychiatrist or a famous author, I'm just a regular person like you who had to live and learn but has just as much knowledge as a doctor or psychiatrist. In writing this guide I would like to say that the information that I'm giving you came from two sources, the first was from reading different books. But as we know books can only give you so much information, so what is the next best thing. I went straight to the source, men. Ladies 99.9% of my book is from observation of men, conversations with men and my own life experiences with men, so damn it listen! What better teacher is there then to get it straight from the horses' mouth. Let me ask you a question, "What would you rather be respected or treasured?" Hmm. I pray you know the difference, if not ask somebody. I want to be treasured because to be treasured, means my partner and I have reached a level of love and understanding beyond anybody's comprehension and nothing can destroy that love. When you are treasured, respect will automatically come. Think about an item that you treasure with all your heart, nobody better not touch it. You will protect it to the very end. It holds a special place in your heart. When you are treasured your roots are very strong. When the roots of a tree are well grounded and are very deep, no storm can come at it and destroy it. Become a tree with strong roots because storms are sure to come and you need to be prepared. Don't get caught short. This guide will set you on your way to be treasured and to help you have strong roots.

God Bless

Dedication

This book is dedicated to all the men that have come into my life whether it be positive or negative for without the experiences I have encountered with you I would not have gained such vast knowledge. The experiences and encounters have helped me to grow as a person and as a Woman. So I say Thank-You!!!!

To my God for if you did not put these men in my life to show me the way none of this would be possible. For without you I am nothing for with you I am everything. Thank-You my God my main man who will never leave me or forsake me.

God is definitely a Keeper!!!!!☺

Acknowledgement

Thank-you to my two wonderful children Tyesha and P.J. I'm glad that God brought you into my life. To my wonderful, energetic granddaughter who all of this is for, for her future, Sugar Baby (Imani). You lift my spirits up every time I see you, even though you get on my last nerve sometimes. I love you so much. I love you all. To my family and friends who believed in my dream and me and supported me on this journey. To my Next Level, MC family, you are a wild bunch of guys and the experiences I have had with you guys money can't buy. I have learned something from each of you. I love you guys. Ooohhh ☺. To "L" Larry Thank-You!! For the wonderful title and countless conversations concerning the writing of this guide and life in general. You kept my mind stimulated. "L" you are a **"Keeper"** quiet as kept. Love you much.

Last but not least to my Sweetie, (Daddy ☺) for without your support, understanding and believing in me I would have not done this. Thank-you for pushing me. Thank-you for being you. You are a hellava man. Regardless of the situation you are definitely a **"Keeper"** don't let no one tell you differently. You have inspired me in so many ways in writing this guide that you don't even know about. You have help to change me in a beautiful way. When no one could hear my silent screams you always heard them and I Thank-you and love you for that. Love 4- Ever and a Day. Now it's your turn to do the damn thing and go for your dreams!! I got your back!!! I will always be by your side.

Hugs & Kisses ☺.

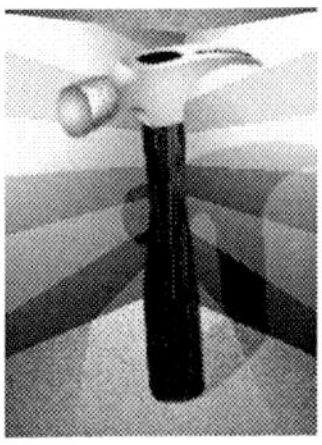

Contents

Reflections

The following list of poems are poems that I call reflections. They are reflections because during some of the hardest times in my life they have helped me to reflect upon things that needed to be changed in my life and get me through the rough spots. They have assisted me on my journey through life and I hope they will become an asset in your journey through life.

The ideas in this book are only for a man you truly feel and know in your heart is worthy of it. "A Keeper", not an abusive man, whether it be physical or mental abuse. Abuse is abuse. Nothing in this book can help him or change him, only God can change him. This book is not to be used to manipulate a man into loving you, it will back fire. The love will not be honest or sincere. Love will never manipulate another person.

Love

Love is patient, love is kind. It does not envy, it does not boast, it is not proud. It is not rude, it is not self-seeking, it is not easily angered, and it keeps no record of wrongs. Love does not delight in evil but rejoices with the truth. It always protects, always trusts, always hopes, and always perseveres. Love never fails. Everybody wants love. Men are no different. Men want all the things we want in love. Love, it nurtures trust and sets a man's heart at rest because love is faithful and loyal. It doesn't compete with him it completes him. In love you have to be flexible.

The ideas in this book are only for a man you truly feel and know in your heart is worthy of it. "A Keeper", not an abusive man, whether it be physical or mental abuse. Abuse is abuse. Nothing in this book can help him or change him, only God can change him. This book is not to be used to manipulate a man into loving you, it will back fire. The love will not be honest or sincere. Love will never manipulate another person.

Happiness

We convince ourselves that life will be better once we get married, have a baby, then another.

Then we get frustrated because our children are not old enough, and that all will be well when they are older.

Then we are frustrated because they reach adolescence and we must deal with them. Surely we'll be happier when they grow out of the teen years.

We tell ourselves our life will be better when our spouse get his/her act together, when we have a nicer car, when we can take a vacation, when we finally retire.

The truth is that there is no better time to be happy than right now. If not, then when? Your life will always be full of challenges. It is better to admit as much and to decide to be happy in spite of it all.

For the longest time, it seemed that life was about to start. Real life. But there was always some obstacle along the way, an ordeal to get through, some work to be finished, some time to be given, a bill to be paid, then life would start. I finally came to understand that those obstacles were life.

That point of view helped me see that there isn't any road to happiness. Happiness is the road.

So, enjoy every moment. Stop waiting for school to end, for a return to school, to lose ten pounds, to gain ten pounds, for work to begin, to get married, for Friday evening, for Sunday morning, waiting for a new car, for your mortgage to be paid off, for spring, for summer, for fall, for winter, for the first or the fifteenth of the month, for your song to be played on the radio, to die, to be reborn... before deciding to be happy.

Happiness is a voyage, not a destination.
There is no better time to be happy than NOW!!
Live and enjoy the moment.
AUTHOR UNKNOWN

The ideas in this book are only for a man you truly feel and know in your heart is worthy of it. "A Keeper", not an abusive man, whether it be physical or mental abuse. Abuse is abuse. Nothing in this book can help him or change him, only God can change him. This book is not to be used to manipulate a man into loving you, it will back fire. The love will not be honest or sincere. Love will never manipulate another person.

Woman to Woman Encouragement

Someone will always be smarter. Their house will be bigger. They will drive a better car. Their children will do better in school. And their partners will fix more things around the house. So let it go and love you and your circumstances. Think about it. The prettiest woman in the world can have hell in her heart. And the most highly favored woman on you job may be unable to have children. The richest woman you know – she's got the car, the house, the clothes – might be heartbreakingly lonely. So, love you. Love who you are right now. Tell yourself, "I am too blessed to be stressed". **"To The World You Might Be One Person, But To One Person You Just Might Be The World".**

AUTHOR UNKNOWN

The ideas in this book are only for a man you truly feel and know in your heart is worthy of it. "A Keeper", not an abusive man, whether it be physical or mental abuse. Abuse is abuse. Nothing in this book can help him or change him, only God can change him. This book is not to be used to manipulate a man into loving you, it will back fire. The love will not be honest or sincere. Love will never manipulate another person.

A Strong Woman
-VS-
A Woman of Strength

A strong woman works out every day to keep her body in shape ... but a woman of strength kneels in prayer to keep her soul in shape...

A strong woman isn't afraid of anything... but a woman of strength shows courage in the midst of her fear...

A strong woman won't let anyone get the best of her... but a woman of strength gives the best of her to everyone...

A strong woman makes mistakes and avoids the same in the future... a woman of strength realizes life's mistakes can also be God's blessings and capitalizes on them...

A strong woman walks sure footedly... but a woman of strength knows God will catch her when she falls...

A strong woman wears the look of confidence on her face... but a woman of strength wears grace...
A strong woman has faith that she is strong enough for the journey... but a woman of strength has faith that it is the journey that she will become strong...Complied by Suka Pasi

The ideas in this book are only for a man you truly feel and know in your heart is worthy of it. "A Keeper", not an abusive man, whether it be physical or mental abuse. Abuse is abuse. Nothing in this book can help him or change him, only God can change him. This book is not to be used to manipulate a man into loving you, it will back fire. The love will not be honest or sincere. Love will never manipulate another person.

If A Man Wants You!!

- *If a man wants you, nothing can keep him away.*

- *If he doesn't want you, nothing can make him stay.*
- *Stop making excuses for a man and his behavior. Allow your intuition (or spirit) to save you from heartache.*
- *Stop trying to change yourselves for a relationship that's not meant to be.*
- *Slower is better. Never live your life for a man before you find what makes you truly happy.*
- *If a relationship ends because the man was not treating you as you deserve then heck no, you can't "be friends". A friend wouldn't mistreat a friend. Don't settle.*
- *Don't stay because you think "it will get better". You'll be mad at yourself a year later for staying when things are not better.*
- *The only person you can control in a relationship is you.*
- *Always have your own set of friends separate from his.*
- *Maintain boundaries in how a guy treats you. If something bothers you, speak up.*
- *Never let a man know everything. He will use it against you later.*

The ideas in this book are only for a man you truly feel and know in your heart is worthy of it. "A Keeper", not an abusive man, whether it be physical or mental abuse. Abuse is abuse. Nothing in this book can help him or change him, only God can change him. This book is not to be used to manipulate a man into loving you, it will back fire. The love will not be honest or sincere. Love will never manipulate another person.

- *You cannot change a man's behavior. Change comes from within.*
- *Don't ever make him feel he is more important than you are even if he has more education or in a better job. Do not make him into a quasi-god. He is a man, nothing more nothing less.*
- *Never let a man define who you are.*
- *A man will only treat you the way you allow him to treat you.*
- *All men are not dogs.*
- *You should not be the one doing all the bending…compromise is a two way street.*
- *You need time to heal between relationships…there is nothing cute about baggage deal with your issues before pursuing a new relationship.*
- *You should never look for someone to complete you…a relationship consists of two whole individuals…look for someone complimentary…not supplementary.*
- *Dating is fun…even if he doesn't turn out to be Mr. Right.*
- *Make him miss you sometimes…when a man always know where you are, and your always readily available to him – he takes it for granted.*

- *Don't fully commit to a man who doesn't give you everything that you need. Keep him in your radar but get to know others.*

They say it takes a minute to find a special person, an hour to appreciate them, a day to love them and an entire lifetime to forget them.

AUTHOR UNKNOWN

The ideas in this book are only for a man you truly feel and know in your heart is worthy of it. "A Keeper", not an abusive man, whether it be physical or mental abuse. Abuse is abuse. Nothing in this book can help him or change him, only God can change him. This book is not to be used to manipulate a man into loving you, it will back fire. The love will not be honest or sincere. Love will never manipulate another person.

Divinely Inspired Victorious Achievers

I Know This Applies To You................
A good woman is proud of herself. She respects herself and others. She is aware of who she is. She neither seeks definitions from the person she is with, or does she expect them to read her mind. She is quite capable of articulating her needs.
A good woman is hopeful. She is strong enough to make all her dreams come true. She know love, therefore she gives love. She recognizes that her love has great value and must be reciprocated. If her love is taken for granted, it soon disappears.

A good woman has a dash of inspiration, a dabble of endurance. She knows that she will, at times have to inspire others to reach the potential God gave them. A good woman knows her past, understands her present and moves toward the future.

A good woman knows God. She knows that with God the world is her playground, but without God she will just be played. A good woman does not live in fear of the future because of her past. Instead, she understands that her life experiences are merely lessons, meant to bring her closer to self knowledge and unconditional self love. Girl Smile!!

The ideas in this book are only for a man you truly feel and know in your heart is worthy of it. "A Keeper", not an abusive man, whether it be physical or mental abuse. Abuse is abuse. Nothing in this book can help him or change him, only God can change him. This book is not to be used to manipulate a man into loving you, it will back fire. The love will not be honest or sincere. Love will never manipulate another person.

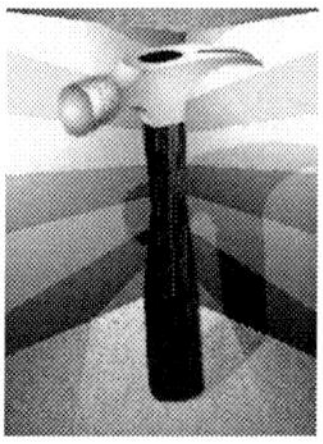

Introduction

What Is A Keeper?

What is a **"Keeper"** and how do you maintain a **"Keeper"**? Well for the first part of this question here is my definition of a **"Keeper"**. A **"Keeper"** is a man who supports you in all of your decisions, a man who uplifts you when you are down, a man who will help you to achieve your dreams, a man who takes care of all his responsibilities as the man of the house. A **"Keeper"** is a provider, protector, lover, friend, confidant, fixer, just a Damn Good Man! A **"Keeper"** is not disrespectful or hurtful intentionally. We are their Queens and they are our Kings. Ladies we all know if we have a **"Keeper"** or not, all we have to do is open our eyes and see the truth. Women we have to **"Maintain our Keepers"** because you know we are special and difficult sometimes and we can mess up a damn good relationship and turn a good man away because we don't or won't understand him.

We as women focus on all the things he is not doing instead on the things he is doing and we don't look at all the positive characteristics he has. We think it's all about us when it's about the partnership between "Man & Woman".

The ideas in this book are only for a man you truly feel and know in your heart is worthy of it. "A Keeper", not an abusive man, whether it be physical or mental abuse. Abuse is abuse. Nothing in this book can help him or change him, only God can change him. This book is not to be used to manipulate a man into loving you, it will back fire. The love will not be honest or sincere. Love will never manipulate another person.

☆☆

The key to love, when imagined by the mind and crafted by the hand, can unlock any door.

Sophia Bedford-Pierce

☆☆

The ideas in this book are only for a man you truly feel and know in your heart is worthy of it. "A Keeper", not an abusive man, whether it be physical or mental abuse. Abuse is abuse. Nothing in this book can help him or change him, only God can change him. This book is not to be used to manipulate a man into loving you, it will back fire. The love will not be honest or sincere. Love will never manipulate another person.

He will try in every way to make you happy in spite of his own happiness and as women we don't seem to get it. We think he is being difficult, he is not listening to us, why doesn't he feel the same way as we do. When sometimes we are the ones not listening and not getting it. Hopefully as you go through the pages of this guide, the journey of **"Maintaining a Keeper"** will be a simple one. Just keep an open mind during the ride. In order to **"Maintain a Keeper"** there are fifteen (15) lessons to be learned and they are: We are the beginning. It starts within us, What do you want, Your place as woman, Communication, Expectations, Individualism, Privacy, Influence, Submission, Consideration/concern/understanding, Intimacy, Past relationships & other relationships, Confrontations, Affair-cheating, and Marriage-partnership. So let's begin the journey to **"Maintain a Keeper"**.

God Bless

The ideas in this book are only for a man you truly feel and know in your heart is worthy of it. "A Keeper", not an abusive man, whether it be physical or mental abuse. Abuse is abuse. Nothing in this book can help him or change him, only God can change him. This book is not to be used to manipulate a man into loving you, it will back fire. The love will not be honest or sincere. Love will never manipulate another person.

☆☆

The key to love unlocks our strongest emotions.

Sophia Bedford-Pierce

☆☆

The ideas in this book are only for a man you truly feel and know in your heart is worthy of it. "A Keeper", not an abusive man, whether it be physical or mental abuse. Abuse is abuse. Nothing in this book can help him or change him, only God can change him. This book is not to be used to manipulate a man into loving you, it will back fire. The love will not be honest or sincere. Love will never manipulate another person.

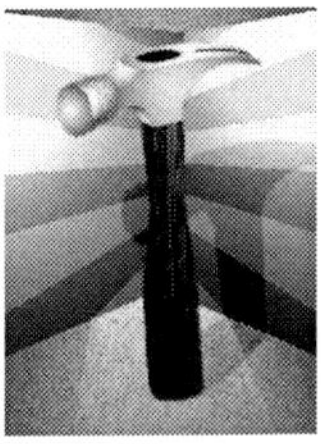

We Are The Beginning. It Starts Within Us.

We are the beginning. It starts within us. When we conceive & birth a child we bring life into the world and that's a beautiful thing. When we start a relationship that man comes to us and we can make it a beautiful thing or an ugly thing. Before we can ever begin to understand and love our men we must and I mean must learn to love and respect ourselves. Once we begin to understand, love and respect ourselves and know what we want it makes life a whole lot easier. We need to see what has to be changed about us if anything. Change is the hardest part about being grown, you have to be willing to look at your life honestly and make the change. Maybe there is something that needs to be added about us or taken away about us. Some of us are over bearing, talkative, nagging, shy, overzealous and the list goes on.

The ideas in this book are only for a man you truly feel and know in your heart is worthy of it. "A Keeper", not an abusive man, whether it be physical or mental abuse. Abuse is abuse. Nothing in this book can help him or change him, only God can change him. This book is not to be used to manipulate a man into loving you, it will back fire. The love will not be honest or sincere. Love will never manipulate another person.

☆☆☆

An authentic love bears no regrets.

Sophia Bedford-Pierce

☆☆☆

The ideas in this book are only for a man you truly feel and know in your heart is worthy of it. "A Keeper", not an abusive man, whether it be physical or mental abuse. Abuse is abuse. Nothing in this book can help him or change him, only God can change him. This book is not to be used to manipulate a man into loving you, it will back fire. The love will not be honest or sincere. Love will never manipulate another person.

We need to see what characteristics that have to be changed that maybe hindering the growth of our relationships or that stops the relationship from coming back together.

A lot of us cannot and will not make the change because it hurts when you look at your life and say damn I f_cked-up but its O.K. to F_ck-up or be F_cked-up as long as you learn from the mistake. But realize that we all make mistakes and how I look at it is that they are experiences not mistakes because I have learned from them and when you don't learn from them, then they stay as mistakes.

Your spirit has to be full of life and energy. That life force will draw people towards you. If you look into your life, you will see that one person that everybody draws to. You have said this or you have heard someone say this before "he or she is just such a beautiful person, their whole disposition is pleasant or beautiful". There is nothing anyone can say bad about that person. No matter what the situation is they always have a smile, always willing to help or have a kind word to say. That is the spirit that just shines through and everyone is attracted to it. It's the beauty inside. You want a spirit like that and not the opposite. We have all encountered the negative, miserable person and what do we do when we encounter this person we run the opposite direction.

☆☆☆

A map of the heart provides the key to the soul.

Sophia Bedford-Pierce

☆☆☆

The ideas in this book are only for a man you truly feel and know in your heart is worthy of it. "A Keeper", not an abusive man, whether it be physical or mental abuse. Abuse is abuse. Nothing in this book can help him or change him, only God can change him. This book is not to be used to manipulate a man into loving you, it will back fire. The love will not be honest or sincere. Love will never manipulate another person.

Don't be the person that your spouse runs away from be the person he comes to. It's a matter of positive versus negative. No matter what is going on in your household always stay positive for it will bring the best out of your relationship. Stay negative and you will get nothing out of your relationship. Yes, I know and God knows I know it's hard to stay positive when all hell is breaking lose but you can do it trust me because, I have done it countless of times. When you stay positive all the answers will come and you can see the situation clearly and your man will recognize the strength and resolve you have in any given situation and he will fall back. Once we have taken care of the inside now lets work on the outside. When you get up in the morning or throughout your day just look at yourself honestly in the mirror and see if you like what you see because this is where it all starts for men, the visual eye candy. I say this because men are visual creatures like we are emotional creatures.

Men love eye candy so we must look at ourselves and see what we can do to improve ourselves, if anything. You maybe just fine the way you are but it doesn't hurt to take a self-analysis. When our men look at us they look at our face and our body. We all have assets that can be enhanced. When you look at your eyes, maybe you could use some eyeliner or mascara or get your eyebrows trimmed to bring out your eyes.

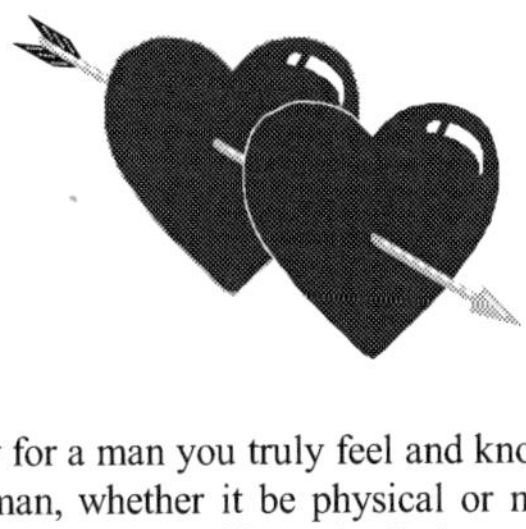

The ideas in this book are only for a man you truly feel and know in your heart is worthy of it. "A Keeper", not an abusive man, whether it be physical or mental abuse. Abuse is abuse. Nothing in this book can help him or change him, only God can change him. This book is not to be used to manipulate a man into loving you, it will back fire. The love will not be honest or sincere. Love will never manipulate another person.

****

Love awakens and enhances all your senses.

Sophia Bedford-Pierce

****

The ideas in this book are only for a man you truly feel and know in your heart is worthy of it. "A Keeper", not an abusive man, whether it be physical or mental abuse. Abuse is abuse. Nothing in this book can help him or change him, only God can change him. This book is not to be used to manipulate a man into loving you, it will back fire. The love will not be honest or sincere. Love will never manipulate another person.

Has a man ever told you that you have beautiful eyes, well that's one asset to be proud of and show it off. Remember the eyes are the windows to the soul. He will either see a sparkle of light or just emptiness. Our lips, the softness of a kiss. Your lips should not be dry and cracked, that doesn't look good on a woman. If you wear lipstick wear a color that will really accentuate your lips not take away from your lips. Some women wear bright red lipstick and they either have very big lips or very small lips and they look like a clown, don't be the clown.

Smile. Always smile it makes people more receptive towards you and it takes more muscles to frown then to smile. Who wants frown wrinkles. A smile shows happiness. Like the sign on the door that says welcome, your smile is the sign that says welcome. Teeth, Oh God if you have a dental plan do use it. Get your teeth cleaned on regular basis, there is nothing like talking to someone with bad breath, that is a complete turn off. If you have a cracked tooth get it fixed that is what dental coverage is for. Yellow stained teeth is just plain ugly. There are so many items on the market to whiten your teeth, it just a small investment. If your teeth are messed up then you can't smile and remember your smile is your welcome sign and it can calm any situation down or heat a situation up (if you know what I mean☺).

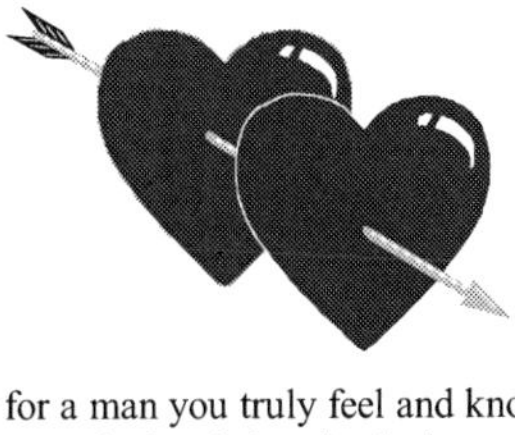

The ideas in this book are only for a man you truly feel and know in your heart is worthy of it. "A Keeper", not an abusive man, whether it be physical or mental abuse. Abuse is abuse. Nothing in this book can help him or change him, only God can change him. This book is not to be used to manipulate a man into loving you, it will back fire. The love will not be honest or sincere. Love will never manipulate another person.

****

Love well and dream with passion.

Sophia Bedford-Pierce

****

The ideas in this book are only for a man you truly feel and know in your heart is worthy of it. "A Keeper", not an abusive man, whether it be physical or mental abuse. Abuse is abuse. Nothing in this book can help him or change him, only God can change him. This book is not to be used to manipulate a man into loving you, it will back fire. The love will not be honest or sincere. Love will never manipulate another person.

Skin care - Get a skin care regiment going on. There are scrubs, moisturizers, etc. out there to help you have beautiful skin. I have found my skin care regiment and it is Apricot Scrub by St. Ives©, cortisone cream and Olay© and I have gotten many compliments on my skin. Oh yeah definitely drink plenty of water, get rid of the stress because stress is something that shows up in the facial area and our diet is what also messes up our skin. What you put in your body will come out in some type of form whether it be good or bad.

Hair - wash your hair on a regular basis at least once a week, go to the beauty parlor and treat yourself to a new do. Nobody wants smelly, oily, dirty hair on their chest or pillow.

Hand and feet - your hands are what will touch him, caress him, hug him and even feed him. Men are visual if you have crusty dry rough hands and dirty nails he doesn't want you to touch or feed him. You don't have to get tips or anything fancy like that, just get a manicure or do it yourself. Your nails should always be clean. Look at some women hands and nails or a man's hand and nails and tell yourself what you think. You won't like what you see out there.

Your feet, we need them point blank so take care of them. Without our feet how would we get around.

The ideas in this book are only for a man you truly feel and know in your heart is worthy of it. "A Keeper", not an abusive man, whether it be physical or mental abuse. Abuse is abuse. Nothing in this book can help him or change him, only God can change him. This book is not to be used to manipulate a man into loving you, it will back fire. The love will not be honest or sincere. Love will never manipulate another person.

****

Finding love should not end your thirst for fulfillment, but serve as a well from which to drink more deeply.

Sophia Bedford-Pierce

****

The ideas in this book are only for a man you truly feel and know in your heart is worthy of it. "A Keeper", not an abusive man, whether it be physical or mental abuse. Abuse is abuse. Nothing in this book can help him or change him, only God can change him. This book is not to be used to manipulate a man into loving you, it will back fire. The love will not be honest or sincere. Love will never manipulate another person.

Pedicures feel good and are beautiful. Clothing, I just have one thing to say and that is everything isn't for everyone in other words what's in style isn't meant for everyone to wear. You should be honest with yourself when you wear something, don't get caught wearing something that is wrong, just plain wrong. Clothing should be sexy for you and your man not the world. See what he likes and try to cater to that desire, if it is appropriate and respectable for you.

MMMM - Scent(perfume) smell is one of the greatest of the five senses. If he likes a particular perfume or scent buy it and buy plenty of it. Whenever he smells that scent it will automatically shock his subconscious mind and he will be thinking of you, I don't care who else wears that fragrance he will think of you. When I smell my Sweetie cologne my mind automatically thinks of him.

Prime example when you smell the scent of a barbecue it just sparks of memories, so start creating beautiful memories with your scent.

Cleanliness, good breath, clean hair, good skin is the first thing he sees in the morning and at night when he lays down to go to sleep, so you should stay on top of your game at all times.

The ideas in this book are only for a man you truly feel and know in your heart is worthy of it. "A Keeper", not an abusive man, whether it be physical or mental abuse. Abuse is abuse. Nothing in this book can help him or change him, only God can change him. This book is not to be used to manipulate a man into loving you, it will back fire. The love will not be honest or sincere. Love will never manipulate another person.

****

One cannot teach how to find love, but it can be learned.

Sophia Bedford-Pierce

****

The ideas in this book are only for a man you truly feel and know in your heart is worthy of it. "A Keeper", not an abusive man, whether it be physical or mental abuse. Abuse is abuse. Nothing in this book can help him or change him, only God can change him. This book is not to be used to manipulate a man into loving you, it will back fire. The love will not be honest or sincere. Love will never manipulate another person.

You can't go to bed every single night with a worn and tattered lingerie or nightgown, hair messed up or a scarf on your head and expect for him to really get it on.

When you tend to look that way every night and he does get it on with you don't be surprised if he is visualizing another woman and he is sleeping with you because it's a matter of convenience. Men are visual creatures. You must keep him looking no matter what because there is a lot of eye candy out there in the world. How you look to catch him is how you have to look to keep him. And finally your posture, you should walk with confidence - shoulders upright, head facing forward and up. Sit upright it shows a silent sense of self and strength. If you are slouching people assume you are weak.

Everything I just spoke about is not just for the man in your life but for you first and foremost because it starts with us and we are the beginning. I feel so much better about myself when I pamper myself.

Cooking - We must get back to cooking (home cook meal). Some of us are into this new age woman crap, girlfriend snap out of it, cook for that man. A way to a man's heart is through his stomach. Men get tired of microwave food and fast food.

****

Sharing the lessons of love can make you a beloved teacher.

Sophia Bedford-Pierce

****

The ideas in this book are only for a man you truly feel and know in your heart is worthy of it. "A Keeper", not an abusive man, whether it be physical or mental abuse. Abuse is abuse. Nothing in this book can help him or change him, only God can change him. This book is not to be used to manipulate a man into loving you, it will back fire. The love will not be honest or sincere. Love will never manipulate another person.

Men want and need to know that they are worth the sweat in the kitchen. Just like when we were kids and mama would sweat in the morning cooking breakfast and sweat at night cooking dinner, we felt good, mama loves us so much to take the time out to feed us and feed us real good.

If he goes to mama house everyday or every other day or on Sundays, you have a problem. Fix the problem girl ask him what he wants for dinner and how he would like it to be cooked and do it. He will beam like damn my woman feeds me damn good and was considerate enough to ask what do I want to eat and make it the way I like it.

When we begin to get ourselves right inside and outside there is less of a chance of us being moody and short tempered. A man can't stand a moody woman. A man likes to know who he is dealing with, one day he has Sybil then Tanya now Linda. If you want a man to leave then keep switching personalities. Men want and need consistency in their life and relationship. Be consistent. Life is full of choices and it's up to us to start making the right choices in our lives. We have to take care of our mind, spirit and body. Men come to our hearts through our faithfulness, sincerity, giving heart, unselfish, unafraid of really being ourselves and most important **uncomplicated**. WE ARE THE BEGINNING. IT STARTS WITHIN US.

The ideas in this book are only for a man you truly feel and know in your heart is worthy of it. "A Keeper", not an abusive man, whether it be physical or mental abuse. Abuse is abuse. Nothing in this book can help him or change him, only God can change him. This book is not to be used to manipulate a man into loving you, it will back fire. The love will not be honest or sincere. Love will never manipulate another person.

☆☆

Inspiration and desire ignite the fires of love.

Sophia Bedford-Pierce

☆☆

The ideas in this book are only for a man you truly feel and know in your heart is worthy of it. "A Keeper", not an abusive man, whether it be physical or mental abuse. Abuse is abuse. Nothing in this book can help him or change him, only God can change him. This book is not to be used to manipulate a man into loving you, it will back fire. The love will not be honest or sincere. Love will never manipulate another person.

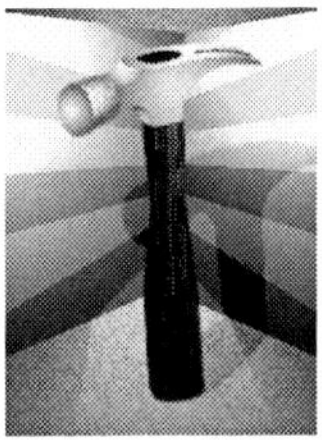

What Do You Really Want?

When you get involved with a man, you have to begin to know what you want in a man and from a man. When I say what you want from a man I mean a relationship, marriage, friendship etc. When coming into a relationship if the man states he does not want a relationship and only wants to be your friend and you know that your are looking for a relationship, "Mr. Right", move on he is not the one for you. You cannot and will not change is mind. Do you want a man, who is sensitive, rough, understanding, kind, aggressive, talkative, etc.? The list of qualities goes on and on. When we don't decide what we want in a man we end up with garbage. When you go shopping and everything looks good and exciting you take it home but then you realize you don't even like the outfit. You are stuck because there is a no return policy, so don't get stuck with someone you really don't want. In knowing what you want in a man, "your Prince Charming" you must know the characteristics you want in a man. To give you some guidance in figuring out what you want in a man here is "My Prince Charming Profile".

Autonomy--I want a partner who will give me space to be my own person.
Sense of humor – I want a partner who is sharp and can enjoy the humorous side of life.

The ideas in this book are only for a man you truly feel and know in your heart is worthy of it. "A Keeper", not an abusive man, whether it be physical or mental abuse. Abuse is abuse. Nothing in this book can help him or change him, only God can change him. This book is not to be used to manipulate a man into loving you, it will back fire. The love will not be honest or sincere. Love will never manipulate another person.

Kindness – I want a partner who is gentle and kind.
Spirituality – I want a partner with the similar deep commitment to spirituality, who shares or understands my beliefs.
Communicator – I want a partner who is good at talking and listening because God knows I love to talk and listen to others. It stimulates my mind and spirit.
Share Interests – I want a partner who is willing to share my interests, passions and definitely my dreams!
Tolerant – I want a partner who is able to hear and appreciate different viewpoints.
Passionate – I must have and I mean must have a partner who is willing to explore our sexual desires with passion and understanding.
Self-Confident – I want a partner who knows and believes in himself throughout life's ups and downs.
Affectionate – I want a partner who is comfortable giving and receiving affection.
Stepchildren – I must have a partner who will accept my children as their own.
Strong Character – I must have a partner who is honest and strong enough to do the right thing no matter the situation.
Dependence – I cannot have a partner who bases his happiness on me. My happiness is based upon me for I am the only one who can make me happy. All my partner can do is add to that happiness, as I will do the same for him.
Rude – I cannot and will not have a partner who is belittling, impatient or hateful to me or other people in any situation.
Punctuality – I can't stand someone who is always late. I don't mind sometimes being late but late all the time it drives me crazy because I try to be on time.

Petty – I will not have a partner who focuses on imperfection because no one is perfect but God
Cynicism – I don't like a person who generally sees the world from a cynical perspective. They find no joy in nothing at all. My motto is if it's that bad then go and kill yourself and spare the rest of us your cynical views who try to see the positive in any given situation. Sorry to be so harsh but it's how I feel.
Childishness – I don't need a partner who is not emotionally mature. We all have that inner child in us that needs to get out once in a while but I'm not here to be my partners' mother he has one already. I will not raise a grown man.
Undependable – Your word is your bond. Don't give me your word if you don't mean it. Which means a lot to me. I mean what I say and I say what I mean. I can't stand a person who fails to come through and is unreliable all the time.
Drugs – What can I say I don't get high and I don't want to be around someone who gets high. I'm not judging but that's not my bag and not something I want to be around.
Depressed – I can't stand a person who is constantly unhappy about their life. Life is full of choices, if you don't like something about your life then change it. You don't have to continue to deal with something you don't like.
Mean Spirited – I will not tolerate a person who has a devious nature and mean to others. Do unto others as you would have others do unto you.

Now ladies, am I being unrealistic? I don't think so. I am asking for too much? I don't think so. I know what I want in my man. Will I get everything, probably not because in any relationship you will compromise and bend just a little to accommodate each other.

☆☆

There are no wrong places in which to look for love-everyone is in some way worthy of receiving it.

Sophia Bedford-Pierce

☆☆

The ideas in this book are only for a man you truly feel and know in your heart is worthy of it. "A Keeper", not an abusive man, whether it be physical or mental abuse. Abuse is abuse. Nothing in this book can help him or change him, only God can change him. This book is not to be used to manipulate a man into loving you, it will back fire. The love will not be honest or sincere. Love will never manipulate another person.

But until that one comes along I have a guideline and I am damn sho nuff going to try and get all the qualities I want in "My Prince Charming". Check out the key word "My Prince Charming". When I say this is that you have to decide what characteristics you want for "Your Prince Charming". Ladies don't play yourself cheap, step your standards up and go for it. It may or may not take a little longer to find that one but it will be worth the wait in the long run. Patience is a virtue. Good things come to those who wait. In knowing what you want, wait on mister right who will fill those shoes. And in waiting don't look at somebody else's mister right. Just because your girlfriend's husband/boyfriend may seem attentive, nice and all that good stuff, just remember you don't live in that household. All the qualities he shows in public are good but in private he is a jackass, so don't compare. Establish your own man in your mind as you meet him and not his representative. So many times we figure a first impression is a lasting impression and it is but when we give a fake impression it will have everybody deceived and now you don't know whom you are dealing with. Be yourself. Everybody is scared to be themselves worrying that he or she won't like them. So what if they don't like the true you then it wasn't meant to be. If you like to eat your food with your hands go for it because that's you. All he can do is accept it or reject it. It is the representative that always sells dreams and gets us into a bad relationship. We end up with the stalker, abuser, lazy, etc. type of man because in the beginning you met Jimmy his representative who did all the talking instead of Timmy who he really is. This also applies to us as women. Our representative just comes out automatically at the beginning and she does her thing.

****

Love is a gift that should neither be given lightly nor taken insincerely.

Sophia Bedford-Pierce

****

The ideas in this book are only for a man you truly feel and know in your heart is worthy of it. "A Keeper", not an abusive man, whether it be physical or mental abuse. Abuse is abuse. Nothing in this book can help him or change him, only God can change him. This book is not to be used to manipulate a man into loving you, it will back fire. The love will not be honest or sincere. Love will never manipulate another person.

She acts all prissy and cute from The Hamptons when well she knows she is a freak from the South Bronx (nc intended). There are freaks in the Hamptons if not more, it's just a matter of being able to relate to the subject.

Example: If you don't cook don't start out cooking and later down the line you really don't like to cook. This is how the drama and bullsh_t starts. Let him be himself and you do the same.

Men are not mind readers. If you never tell him he will never know. We as women have to tell men what we expect and also ask them what they expect out of the relationship right from the beginning not 10 months down the line when it is too late and he doesn't and he won't understand what the big fuss is all about at that point and you and him will always argue about whatever the issue is.

Once you start understanding what you want you won't end up in fairytale land. There is no real prince charming riding on the white horse to save you as the damsel in distress. Just the men that we love with a whole bunch of faults that we have to live with just like they live with our faults. When we get into fantasy land it gets us into trouble all the time. We want the big house with the white picket fence with the 2.5 kids in the suburbs and we will put unnecessary pressure on him to achieve this when at the time all he can afford is a one(1) bedroom apartment with no kids in the inner city. Too much TV watching of fantasy families that are not real but we fall for that bullsh_t all the time, which isn't real.

☆☆

Love enters lightly on the wings of the soul.

Sophia Bedford-Pierce

☆☆

The ideas in this book are only for a man you truly feel and know in your heart is worthy of it. "A Keeper", not an abusive man, whether it be physical or mental abuse. Abuse is abuse. Nothing in this book can help him or change him, only God can change him. This book is not to be used to manipulate a man into loving you, it will back fire. The love will not be honest or sincere. Love will never manipulate another person.

When knowing what you want you must realize that a man cannot satisfy you. You must come to him already fulfilled. All he should do is add to your life.

When you are complete with your self you find that you will be much more happier with yourself and your mate. Too many woman look for a man to satisfy them and make them happy and they don't realize that only God and they themselves can do that. This is why there are so many unhappy women out there looking and seeking outside of themselves instead of looking inside where it already exists. If you cannot be happy without your partner, you won't be happy together, now check that out. When you know what you want, watch and see how much more complete you will be and closer to obtaining these goals. Don't live to just make him happy, make yourself happy also. Women get so caught up in making a man happy that we forget about ourselves and then we become very miserable and bitter people because he didn't respond the way we wanted him to. It becomes a balance between him and you. We don't allow him to be the man, we took the lead and ran with it, just overbearing and smothering forgetting about ourselves.

Security in our relationships is important in knowing what you want. You must be secure with yourself and your relationship. If you and him are walking down the street let him look at other women. So what God gave him eyes to see. Don't you rather have him looking at women then at men and besides it takes the power out of it.

The ideas in this book are only for a man you truly feel and know in your heart is worthy of it. "A Keeper", not an abusive man, whether it be physical or mental abuse. Abuse is abuse. Nothing in this book can help him or change him, only God can change him. This book is not to be used to manipulate a man into loving you, it will back fire. The love will not be honest or sincere. Love will never manipulate another person.

****

Do not try to coax love from its secret place; your love will rise from within you in its own time.

Sophia Bedford-Pierce

****

The ideas in this book are only for a man you truly feel and know in your heart is worthy of it. "A Keeper", not an abusive man, whether it be physical or mental abuse. Abuse is abuse. Nothing in this book can help him or change him, only God can change him. This book is not to be used to manipulate a man into loving you, it will back fire. The love will not be honest or sincere. Love will never manipulate another person.

If he knows it will bother you then he will sneak and do it anyway or he will do it to piss you off but if you accept it with no problem what can he say then.

What my partner and myself do is point out the different women to each other, it's like a game to us. I don't care as long as he is not gawking, now that would be disrespectful. It's just eye candy and we as women like eye candy also. When we learn ourselves then we can learn a man.

Unconditional love. No such thing with our mates only with our children. You must have conditions and express those conditions on what you will and will not accept and stick to it no matter what and no matter how much it may hurt. Example; if your man hits you or gets high and you don't approve of this type of sh_t and I hope you don't approve of it, but anyway you have to express those conditions and stick to it and say you will not hit me or get high. If you don't abide by that then I will leave you or put you out.

When setting up conditions there are boundaries and I mean realist boundaries for him to understand. Example: In the house before the sun comes up. You know the old saying "don't let the sun catch you coming in." Ridiculous boundary, "I want you back home by 1 AM" now that is bullsh_t for a grown ass man.

The ideas in this book are only for a man you truly feel and know in your heart is worthy of it. "A Keeper", not an abusive man, whether it be physical or mental abuse. Abuse is abuse. Nothing in this book can help him or change him, only God can change him. This book is not to be used to manipulate a man into loving you, it will back fire. The love will not be honest or sincere. Love will never manipulate another person.

☆☆

Whom you choose to love speaks of what you admire in yourself and others.

Sophia Bedford-Pierce

☆☆

The ideas in this book are only for a man you truly feel and know in your heart is worthy of it. "A Keeper", not an abusive man, whether it be physical or mental abuse. Abuse is abuse. Nothing in this book can help him or change him, only God can change him. This book is not to be used to manipulate a man into loving you, it will back fire. The love will not be honest or sincere. Love will never manipulate another person.

You know what happens when you set ridiculous boundaries he will just rebel and give you the opposite. Think about some ridiculous boundary you may have set up in your lifetime and remember the response you got and realized that it didn't work. They are GROWN ASS MEN!!! When we look at our men we know what we got in a man. If he was a frog when you met him he will be a frog in the end. If he was a street runner then he will be a street runner until he is tired not until you are tired, just love him and pray for him and God will change what needs to be changed not you. If he really and truly cares about you then he will truly try his damnest to accommodate your wishes. You have to ask yourself are you really in love with this man? Or do you just love him? Do you know the differencc? Does he know the difference? There is a very big difference. Being in love with someone is respect and unconditional love on both parts. I know I said there is no such thing as unconditional love but this is when you accept that your mate snores, doesn't dress well, overweight, four fingers, a little penis, stutters, always late and you still love this person regardless of their flaws. This is unconditional love. I never stop being me and you love me for who I am no matter what nobody says. We love our friends, family, pets, etc. Ladies know what you want. When you know what you want it will make the journey of any relationship a whole lot easier with less complications.

****

Few sunrises are greeted as eagerly as those viewed through the eyes of love.

Sophia Bedford-Pierce

****

The ideas in this book are only for a man you truly feel and know in your heart is worthy of it. "A Keeper", not an abusive man, whether it be physical or mental abuse. Abuse is abuse. Nothing in this book can help him or change him, only God can change him. This book is not to be used to manipulate a man into loving you, it will back fire. The love will not be honest or sincere. Love will never manipulate another person.

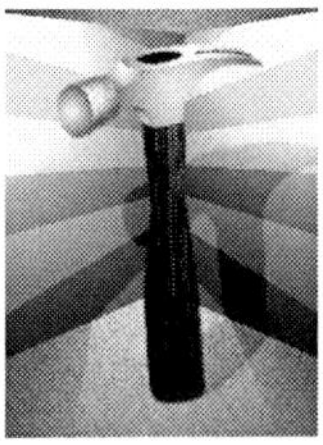

Your Place As A Woman

I know the title of this chapter will have a whole lot of women with their panties in a bunch, well calm down and read on and then you will understand that everybody has a part to play and a place in this game of life and relationships. We as women have to learn or relearn our place as women as God meant it to be. We are mans helpmeet, not his dictator or leader. It is important for a man to lead. If you make a man your ally, he will never be your enemy. You have to be willing to let a man be a man. No man will ever embrace something in which he feels he is in competition with. No man is going to come to a woman where he feels she is always in charge. Men are fixers by nature. If there is nothing for them to fix, they move on in search of unconquered territory. He moves on because you have everything under control and he feels what's the use of me being here, she is the man and woman. You know what affects a man? That is to meet a woman who has womanly qualities.

Choose whom you love with the wisdom of experience, but do not be afraid to celebrate your love with the joy of a child.

Sophia Bedford-Pierce

The ideas in this book are only for a man you truly feel and know in your heart is worthy of it. "A Keeper", not an abusive man, whether it be physical or mental abuse. Abuse is abuse. Nothing in this book can help him or change him, only God can change him. This book is not to be used to manipulate a man into loving you, it will back fire. The love will not be honest or sincere. Love will never manipulate another person.

Men love seeing and experiencing a woman being a woman, it turns them on. As a wife/woman the man in your life should feel his heart, his secrets and his emotions are safe with you. You are supposed to be the one to contribute to regulating his emotions, decisions, cooling him down when he is pissed beyond pisstivity if there is such a word and stirring up his ambitions and passions when the time calls for it. You are supposed to be his safe haven from all the inconsistencies of the world, the one he can always count on. He knows what to expect from you because your personality, character and spirit is in tact. He should not come home every day to find a different woman who he can't figure out who is living in his home. We know our personality sometimes change on a regular basis so let's try to minimize it for his sake and the sake of the relationship.

He is supposed to have access to your heart, your softness, and your reassurances all the time. You are to his oasis. He is supposed to be refreshed in your presence like a breath of fresh air. You are the caregiver of the home. You should be the balance when he comes home. You are the mother of the house. We set the mood as soon as he walks through the door. This is part of your place as the woman of the house. If your home is in chaos then he will not want to come home.

The ideas in this book are only for a man you truly feel and know in your heart is worthy of it. "A Keeper", not an abusive man, whether it be physical or mental abuse. Abuse is abuse. Nothing in this book can help him or change him, only God can change him. This book is not to be used to manipulate a man into loving you, it will back fire. The love will not be honest or sincere. Love will never manipulate another person.

★★

In the court of love, be ever ready to plead your suit.

Sophia Bedford-Pierce

★★

The ideas in this book are only for a man you truly feel and know in your heart is worthy of it. "A Keeper", not an abusive man, whether it be physical or mental abuse. Abuse is abuse. Nothing in this book can help him or change him, only God can change him. This book is not to be used to manipulate a man into loving you, it will back fire. The love will not be honest or sincere. Love will never manipulate another person.

Nothing on earth affects a man like the softness of a woman, his woman. As your place as your mans' woman when he has company over be a good hostess. Always make him feel like the king when he is in front of his friends. You are not there to entertain or have long drawn out conversations with them. If you so choose to do that it will eventually lead to some problems and as we know men are men whether or not they are your partners' friend or not. Leave no room for misunderstanding. They may not know your are playing your part as your partners woman and helping him for a minute because this is something they don't get at home or they are not use to a woman paying attention to them in this manner. To avoid any misunderstanding just ask your partner what he wants you to provide and then do it and disappear.

When you know your place as a woman it makes you strong but don't be strong and wrong. Many of us have had to eat crow because we were so strong about a certain situation but in the long run ended up apologizing or looking stupid. Think ladies before you act. My foot has been put in my mouth on several occasions but I'm getting better at it.

The ideas in this book are only for a man you truly feel and know in your heart is worthy of it. "A Keeper", not an abusive man, whether it be physical or mental abuse. Abuse is abuse. Nothing in this book can help him or change him, only God can change him. This book is not to be used to manipulate a man into loving you, it will back fire. The love will not be honest or sincere. Love will never manipulate another person.

★★

You will be able to give love when you are certain of your own qualities.

Sophia Bedford-Pierce

★★

The ideas in this book are only for a man you truly feel and know in your heart is worthy of it. "A Keeper", not an abusive man, whether it be physical or mental abuse. Abuse is abuse. Nothing in this book can help him or change him, only God can change him. This book is not to be used to manipulate a man into loving you, it will back fire. The love will not be honest or sincere. Love will never manipulate another person.

A man needs to know that if he is unable to take care of a situation that you can and will step in to pick up the slack and not be so head strong and not listen. It gives him reassurance. In knowing this he knows you are not helpless. No man wants a helpless woman. No man wants a helpless woman and the key word is man. A helpless woman will drain him just like a helpless man will drain you. In being strong we have to learn to be vulnerable not weak but able to show we need help, can you help me? The damsel in distress. Remember men are fixers, and it gives them a sense of pride to be able to help.

Enjoy being a woman. It's the most beautiful thing in the world to stand tall, look, feel and smell good. Being feminine adds softness to you. Men love softness and pretty. We are not men so stop trying to take his place for he cannot take your place.

☆☆

Solitude may befriend a thinker, but love becomes fuller when it is shared.

Sophia Bedford-Pierce

☆☆

The ideas in this book are only for a man you truly feel and know in your heart is worthy of it. "A Keeper", not an abusive man, whether it be physical or mental abuse. Abuse is abuse. Nothing in this book can help him or change him, only God can change him. This book is not to be used to manipulate a man into loving you, it will back fire. The love will not be honest or sincere. Love will never manipulate another person.

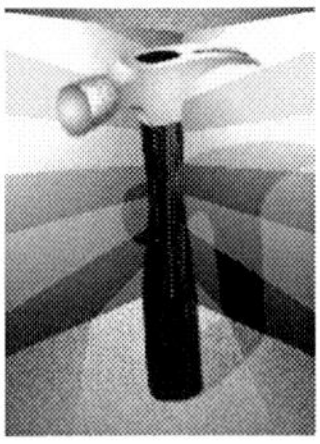

Communication!!!!!

You may say I communicate all the time he just doesn't listen but I bet if a vote was taken most men would say we don't communicate, all we do is talk, talk, nag, nag, talk and never listen. And you know what's crazy, I would have to agree with them. We talk and never really listen to them because if we did we would have a better understanding of his heart and its desires. We have to learn to communicate in his language. Your man may not say a lot, but his actions speak volumes. It's hard to explain but you have to really listen to your mate then you will learn to communicate in his language. William July once said "If your partner is hesitant to talk or is not very emotional, just let him express himself in his own way. Men are always communicating how they really feel-- you just have to read the signs." When you communicate in his language then you begin to understand him much better. When communicating his opinion counts.

The ideas in this book are only for a man you truly feel and know in your heart is worthy of it. "A Keeper", not an abusive man, whether it be physical or mental abuse. Abuse is abuse. Nothing in this book can help him or change him, only God can change him. This book is not to be used to manipulate a man into loving you, it will back fire. The love will not be honest or sincere. Love will never manipulate another person.

****

You cannot command someone to love you. Offering glimpses of the inner you, however, will cause someone to seek you out.

Sophia Bedford-Pierce

****

The ideas in this book are only for a man you truly feel and know in your heart is worthy of it. "A Keeper", not an abusive man, whether it be physical or mental abuse. Abuse is abuse. Nothing in this book can help him or change him, only God can change him. This book is not to be used to manipulate a man into loving you, it will back fire. The love will not be honest or sincere. Love will never manipulate another person.

Ask for his opinion and listen to it and respect it even if you disagree, agree to disagree and he will be ready to open up about a lot of other things in your relationship and life.

We have to listen to learn and learn to listen. If you don't understand that statement then read it again and again until it sinks in. Do not nag. Do not nag. He is not listening when you do this. It's a waste of time. They know how to block us out. You sound like the teacher from Charlie Brown©, Wha, Wha, Wha, get it.

In your relationship you should be able to talk about any and everything no matter what. If you cannot then there is a problem. When a man feels that all you are going to do is criticize or complain, he begins to shut down and not talk at all because he feels you don't respect what he has to say and you are not listening. When trying to keep the lines of communication open you should be well versed on an array of subjects. You should have some knowledge about cars, sports, money, politics, TV shows, music, women and yes, even women. Once the sex is over men want a woman whom they can talk to about a variety of subjects, their subjects not ours all the time. We know our subjects are hair, nails, children, clothes, shopping, and of course gossip. They will have conversations on our subjects for a minute but it is boring to them and they want us to have an interest in their subjects as well.

The ideas in this book are only for a man you truly feel and know in your heart is worthy of it. "A Keeper", not an abusive man, whether it be physical or mental abuse. Abuse is abuse. Nothing in this book can help him or change him, only God can change him. This book is not to be used to manipulate a man into loving you, it will back fire. The love will not be honest or sincere. Love will never manipulate another person.

☆☆

Too much time spent lamenting a love not found leaves too little time to find your heart's desire.

Sophia Bedford-Pierce

☆☆

The ideas in this book are only for a man you truly feel and know in your heart is worthy of it. "A Keeper", not an abusive man, whether it be physical or mental abuse. Abuse is abuse. Nothing in this book can help him or change him, only God can change him. This book is not to be used to manipulate a man into loving you, it will back fire. The love will not be honest or sincere. Love will never manipulate another person.

You see when their buddies are not around you can still stimulate his mind and keep his interests. He will then talk to you about a lot of subjects and you will see how much closer you will become by talking about those simple subjects.

He is sharing ladies and we want them to share with us and not with the other woman remember. When you listen to his feelings and emotions, he is sharing when you least expect it. We as women let our feelings and emotions right out. "I am here so talk to me, I need to talk, I have a problem". Men are the complete opposite. Men will shut down. If you have patience and just ask what's the matter and he says, I had a f_ck-up day, your response should be what happened and if he says I don't want to talk about it then say no problem baby, I'm here if you want to talk, I got you. Eventually he will start to share and share a whole lot. And most importantly if he does share do not and I mean do not give your opinion unless he asks for it and don't criticize him for he will surely shut down real quick on you. Men are truly different species. But if you listen you will learn. When speaking to your man your words should be sweet, honey to his ears not harsh and mean spirited but soft tones.

Ask how was your day? This statement goes a long way and is appreciated by a lot of men.

☆☆

Denying love may diminish the hurt, but it also diminishes the heart.

Sophia Bedford-Pierce

☆☆

The ideas in this book are only for a man you truly feel and know in your heart is worthy of it. "A Keeper", not an abusive man, whether it be physical or mental abuse. Abuse is abuse. Nothing in this book can help him or change him, only God can change him. This book is not to be used to manipulate a man into loving you, it will back fire. The love will not be honest or sincere. Love will never manipulate another person.

When you need your man to do something don't tell him to do it, ask him then he feels he has an option and you are not trying to control him. Remember men are competitors and expect confrontation at any given moment.

Compliments–men love compliments also. Tell him he looks good, smells good and watch how he beams. Encourage him. Encouragement gives him that sense of confidence when he needs it most; it lets him know that you believe in him.

When he does things around the house even though they are little things show delight in the words you speak, like wow baby thank you for putting up that picture, thank you for putting the clothes away, it makes him feel appreciated. Unfortunately, we focus on the things we don't have and what he didn't do that we lose focus on the things we have and all the wonderful things he has done. Silence–know when to speak and when to hold your tongue. When you learn to be silent you will learn a lot. A lot is being said verbally or non-verbally. We tend to run off at our mouths and end up regretting it later. Desire–just like we want our men to desire us they want us to desire them. You can show him how much you desire him by a simple "Hi, honey " like the purring of a cat sends that subliminal message that I want you.

The ideas in this book are only for a man you truly feel and know in your heart is worthy of it. "A Keeper", not an abusive man, whether it be physical or mental abuse. Abuse is abuse. Nothing in this book can help him or change him, only God can change him. This book is not to be used to manipulate a man into loving you, it will back fire. The love will not be honest or sincere. Love will never manipulate another person.

☆☆☆

Where love is a welcomed sign there are no immovable barriers.

Sophia Bedford-Pierce

☆☆☆

The ideas in this book are only for a man you truly feel and know in your heart is worthy of it. "A Keeper", not an abusive man, whether it be physical or mental abuse. Abuse is abuse. Nothing in this book can help him or change him, only God can change him. This book is not to be used to manipulate a man into loving you, it will back fire. The love will not be honest or sincere. Love will never manipulate another person.

Show that man he is desirable by even touching him, kissing him or a simple smile will get his blood to boiling and it will make him feel like king in your world. Instead of waiting for him to initiate sex just grab him and tell him "I want you" and take his clothes off. He will enjoy this and the sex will be explosive. That desire will have him so wired up.

There is something special about a woman who masters the art of gently leading her man to see reason and to make wise decisions for her house. It's not about manipulation. It's about communication. Wisdom keeps the house in order and covers it from all forces that threaten to destroy it.

It's a woman with an open mind to all things that will have a strong relationship that will enable her to see clearly and understand through any given situation. When your mind is more open to all things then your man will be willing to express more without feeling the need to hide or just not share at all with you. The lines of communication will always be open. These are my seven truths that make a relationship withstand the storms of life and its trial and tribulations. Communication, knowledge, discretion, sound judgment, understanding, wisdom and listening.

The ideas in this book are only for a man you truly feel and know in your heart is worthy of it. "A Keeper", not an abusive man, whether it be physical or mental abuse. Abuse is abuse. Nothing in this book can help him or change him, only God can change him. This book is not to be used to manipulate a man into loving you, it will back fire. The love will not be honest or sincere. Love will never manipulate another person.

☆☆

Let your love move with the lightness of air and shine with the intensity of the sun.

Sophia Bedford-Pierce

☆☆

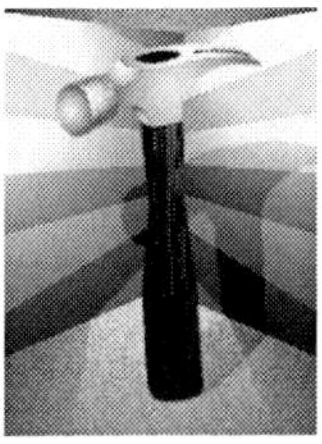

Expectations

Do you remember those velvet posters that were around when we were kids and they had all the astrological signs, black power and a variety of others. All our parents had them on their walls but for me therc was one that always stuck in my mind. Now I don't know the whole thing but this simple statement has stuck with me for over thirty (30) years and it goes like this " I'm not in this world to live up to your expectations and you are not in this world to live up to mine but if we happen to meet then it's a beautiful thing". Expectations we all have them, some are reasonable while others are out of this world, unrealistic and unreasonable. Expectations set us up for resentment with our partners when things don't go the way ***we*** expect them too. Sometimes we get to feeling ignored by our spouses not really understanding or knowing that God could be talking to that man about you. God might be making plans to bless us big-time but because of our own insecurity and expectations we sometimes don't get to see the plans that lie on the heart of the man in our lives.

****

It matters little if the gold cup is finely made and glitters when polished, if it proves to be empty when placed to your lips.

Sophia Bedford-Pierce

****

We stop them from coming to fruition with our own low expectations, misconceived notions and the actions that sometimes follow.

So that man in your life isn't doing what you think he should be doing, your expectation. The key word is what you think. Get out of that mode of thinking. You have prayed and prayed and it seems as if he and God have a conspiracy against you because boyfriend is not changing. Perhaps your expecting him to change and God is waiting for you to change. Remember God uses all relationships to shape and mold us to instill integrity and strength of character within. So expect to be stretched beyond belief and check yourself before you start leveling blame. You can't see the whole picture. You don't have the full blue print for what God is doing to you through you or him. Stop looking at your mate and seeing him as the man who doesn't meet your expectations and instead see him as a man who's doing the best he can. **You know what's funny? Most men don't have a bunch of expectations when it comes to women. ALL THEY WANT IS A WOMAN WHO CAN COOK, SEW, CLEAN, SEX THEM GOOD, RESPECT THEM AND THEIR DECISIONS AND LEAVE THEM BE WHEN THEY WANT TO BE LEFT ALONE.** They just kind of take things as they come.

The ideas in this book are only for a man you truly feel and know in your heart is worthy of it. "A Keeper", not an abusive man, whether it be physical or mental abuse. Abuse is abuse. Nothing in this book can help him or change him, only God can change him. This book is not to be used to manipulate a man into loving you, it will back fire. The love will not be honest or sincere. Love will never manipulate another person.

☆☆

There may be detours on the road to love, but you can reach your destination nonetheless.

Sophia Bedford-Pierce

☆☆

The ideas in this book are only for a man you truly feel and know in your heart is worthy of it. "A Keeper", not an abusive man, whether it be physical or mental abuse. Abuse is abuse. Nothing in this book can help him or change him, only God can change him. This book is not to be used to manipulate a man into loving you, it will back fire. The love will not be honest or sincere. Love will never manipulate another person.

As along as nothing rocks the boat and causes drama in their world, they are O.K. But women come loaded down with all kinds of expectations on how the man should behave and what he should do. We expect him to be the superhuman kind of person when he is only a simple man.

We expect him to work, clean up, pay the bills, help with the children, spend time with us, fix up the house, go with us places whenever we want to go and when one of these expectations falls through now here comes the drama. We nag the sh_t out of him because he didn't do what we expected him to do. But he did do something but it wasn't good enough for us! Ladies we do it all the time. We just complain, complain and are never satisfied. We set ourselves up and we don't even recognize or realize it.

How does a woman give away a man? By giving him what she thinks he needs and expects, instead of what he says he wants and expects. This is why it is of utmost importance to listen to your man and ladies men mean exactly what they say. Yes means yes and no means no and I don't like that means I don't like that. They are not like us where no means no for now and is subject to change. Unfortunately, for everything you won't do for your man there is a woman who understands and listens and is waiting in the wings who is perfectly ready and willing to accommodate his unmet desires and requests. And what does any starving person do when food is placed in front of him? He eats. And there you have the clean up woman. The wisest question a woman can ask her man is what do you want?

The ideas in this book are only for a man you truly feel and know in your heart is worthy of it. "A Keeper", not an abusive man, whether it be physical or mental abuse. Abuse is abuse. Nothing in this book can help him or change him, only God can change him. This book is not to be used to manipulate a man into loving you, it will back fire. The love will not be honest or sincere. Love will never manipulate another person.

****

Everyone should carefully observe with all his strength.

Chassidic Proverb

****

The ideas in this book are only for a man you truly feel and know in your heart is worthy of it. "A Keeper", not an abusive man, whether it be physical or mental abuse. Abuse is abuse. Nothing in this book can help him or change him, only God can change him. This book is not to be used to manipulate a man into loving you, it will back fire. The love will not be honest or sincere. Love will never manipulate another person.

Wisdom is wise because it listens. Listen to the man in your life. Find out what he wants and then give it to him. It keeps outside forces from destroying your home, your relationship and your heart. It's the little bits and pieces falling through the crevices of everyday life that ruin things so pay attention. The accumulation of request ignored. The belittling of his needs and desires because of your expectations. Don't fall short.

The ideas in this book are only for a man you truly feel and know in your heart is worthy of it. "A Keeper", not an abusive man, whether it be physical or mental abuse. Abuse is abuse. Nothing in this book can help him or change him, only God can change him. This book is not to be used to manipulate a man into loving you, it will back fire. The love will not be honest or sincere. Love will never manipulate another person.

****

The glory of friendship is not in the out stretched hand, nor the kindly smile, nor the joy of companionship. It is the spiritual inspiration that comes to one when he discovers someone else believes and is willing to trust him.

Ralph Waldo Emerson

****

The ideas in this book are only for a man you truly feel and know in your heart is worthy of it. "A Keeper", not an abusive man, whether it be physical or mental abuse. Abuse is abuse. Nothing in this book can help him or change him, only God can change him. This book is not to be used to manipulate a man into loving you, it will back fire. The love will not be honest or sincere. Love will never manipulate another person.

Individualism

You are you, I am me and He is him. Being an individual is what makes the world go round and make it a beautiful place to be. We have a variety of personalities to contend with, imagine if we were all the same, damn this world would be a boring place to be. When dealing with a relationship you have to remain an individual, yes you do come together as one on certain issues but to maintain your own sanity never stop living and never expect him to stop living. When I say this I mean if you love to roller skate why should you stop doing it because you got married or you live with someone. I don't think so. Just like if he has his Friday night Poker game let him do him if it makes him happy.

If we are forced to suppress the things we like to do before we met our partners then we live to regret it in the long run and we begin to dislike or despise our partners.

****

Think not you can direct the course of love, for love, if it finds you worthy, directs your course.

Kahil Gibran

****

The ideas in this book are only for a man you truly feel and know in your heart is worthy of it. "A Keeper", not an abusive man, whether it be physical or mental abuse. Abuse is abuse. Nothing in this book can help him or change him, only God can change him. This book is not to be used to manipulate a man into loving you, it will back fire. The love will not be honest or sincere. Love will never manipulate another person.

If you need a man to make you a complete individual then you need to check yourself, for he cannot and I repeat cannot make you a complete individual. That is something you should already an individual.

If you are not then you become needy, greedy, and smothering. When you become one of the above you will push that man away. He will run to his friends, another woman, alcohol, drugs, gambling, just to get away from you and breath. Then in our lives it becomes, I should've, could've would've but I didn't get to accomplish the things ***I*** wanted to do, so what the f_ck. Now everybody is frustrated. Individualism is so important for everyone in a relationship in order for it to last the test of time.

Why do you think people who have been married for thirty(30) years end up divorcing? They divorce because they wanted to be an individual again, something they have been longing for, for a long time. They stop being themselves. They became wrapped into one another. Always continue to do the things you love and allow him to do the same, never stop being yourself and he should never stop being himself. Realize as an individual you cannot control or change him. Change only comes after he sees it and allows it not you nagging him about it. Women are always trying to mold or change a man to their liking and all it does is backfire in your face, accept him.

****

Love makes time pass. Time makes love pass.

Euripides

****

The ideas in this book are only for a man you truly feel and know in your heart is worthy of it. "A Keeper", not an abusive man, whether it be physical or mental abuse. Abuse is abuse. Nothing in this book can help him or change him, only God can change him. This book is not to be used to manipulate a man into loving you, it will back fire. The love will not be honest or sincere. Love will never manipulate another person.

When being in a relationship with a man you have to maintain a variety of interest. If your world evolves around him and you don't have a variety of interest then all you will do is drive yourself and him insane. You start worrying about what he is doing and where he is at, but if you have things on the ball then that's less sh_t off your mind concerning him. We have all been there where all we do is think about that man all the time and it's crazy. Focus your attention elsewhere.

I find that when women are in a relationship they want to know all of his friends. Why? I ask why? More unnecessary nonsense on the brain to worry about. If he wants you to know them then allow him to bring you around or introduce you to those individuals. It's about space. Being an individual. We all want space. When I'm with my friends I'm with them. I don't know about you but I need space and I know that ***all men want and need space of their own. They are screaming for it, just listen and you will hear him loud and clear. Remember actions speak louder than words.*** That is his world. Let him live and when you do he will appreciate it. Men need to bond with other men. Not with their woman all the damn time. You see what really helps in your relationship is when you are aware of your own personal purpose in life which is essential before really settling down with a person. Understanding you. Understanding the concept of being an individual.

The ideas in this book are only for a man you truly feel and know in your heart is worthy of it. "A Keeper", not an abusive man, whether it be physical or mental abuse. Abuse is abuse. Nothing in this book can help him or change him, only God can change him. This book is not to be used to manipulate a man into loving you, it will back fire. The love will not be honest or sincere. Love will never manipulate another person.

Your vision will become clear only when you look into your heart. Who looks outside, dreams. Who looks inside, awakens.

Carl Jung

The ideas in this book are only for a man you truly feel and know in your heart is worthy of it. "A Keeper", not an abusive man, whether it be physical or mental abuse. Abuse is abuse. Nothing in this book can help him or change him, only God can change him. This book is not to be used to manipulate a man into loving you, it will back fire. The love will not be honest or sincere. Love will never manipulate another person.

Privacy

My business is my business and your business is your business. Stop sharing your business, it can be detrimental to your relationship. Do not place family and friends into your relationship. This is the mistake a lot of people make and their relationship suffers drastically. It's real easy to call family and friends to complain and they are willing to listen and give their opinion but not their honest opinion because they are on your side. You will only find a few friends and family members who will give their honest opinion on what they feel you have done wrong (if anything). Family and friends will add nonsense to your relationship and now mama doesn't like you and sister don't like him. And sometimes family may want you to break up because they are miserable. A strong household works out their problems together not with outsiders. Outsiders should only become involved in your private affairs when absolutely necessary.

The ideas in this book are only for a man you truly feel and know in your heart is worthy of it. "A Keeper", not an abusive man, whether it be physical or mental abuse. Abuse is abuse. Nothing in this book can help him or change him, only God can change him. This book is not to be used to manipulate a man into loving you, it will back fire. The love will not be honest or sincere. Love will never manipulate another person.

****

Foundation of a Soul Mate.

Friendship,

Honor,

Trust,

Respect,

Spontaneity,

Affection,

Love

****

The ideas in this book are only for a man you truly feel and know in your heart is worthy of it. "A Keeper", not an abusive man, whether it be physical or mental abuse. Abuse is abuse. Nothing in this book can help him or change him, only God can change him. This book is not to be used to manipulate a man into loving you, it will back fire. The love will not be honest or sincere. Love will never manipulate another person.

Once you tell them your business now Aunt Mae knows, Cousin Jethro knows and then the whole family now knows. Whatever you were trying to work out won't work out. Your man is now alienated and will shut down.

Ninety-five percent of the men are private people. They like privacy.

If you co-mingle with this friends wives, girlfriends, lovers, etc., do not exchange numbers because if you do when her man isn't home she will call your house to see if both spouses are together and if your man is home it's drama or if your man is not home either it can really start some bullsh_t. You will find yourself accusing him of doing wrong and then come to find out he was at his mother's house, stayed late at work or was stranded on the BQE but now you have drama in your house because someone else has drama in their house.

Do not have conversations about your man, their man or any man for that matter because it has away of getting back. If you do be sure it won't get back to your man in a negative way. Pillow talk is a motherf_cker, so know who you are having conversations with because remember misery loves company. A true friend will only listen and only give their opinion when asked and not before. Their concern should be for you and not the relationship. My best friend in the whole wide world had been through a lot in a relationship when we were younger and I never and I mean never gave my opinion or judged her for her decision that she made to stay with that particular gentleman. It was her life and I was there if she needed a support system.

The ideas in this book are only for a man you truly feel and know in your heart is worthy of it. "A Keeper", not an abusive man, whether it be physical or mental abuse. Abuse is abuse. Nothing in this book can help him or change him, only God can change him. This book is not to be used to manipulate a man into loving you, it will back fire. The love will not be honest or sincere. Love will never manipulate another person.

☆☆

It is not our purpose to become each other, it is to recognize each other, to learn and see the other and honor him for what he is.

Hermann Hesse

☆☆

The ideas in this book are only for a man you truly feel and know in your heart is worthy of it. "A Keeper", not an abusive man, whether it be physical or mental abuse. Abuse is abuse. Nothing in this book can help him or change him, only God can change him. This book is not to be used to manipulate a man into loving you, it will back fire. The love will not be honest or sincere. Love will never manipulate another person.

That is what a true friend does. And you know what she never gave her opinion or criticize my decisions on the relationships I have had in my life and we love and respect one another for that. A true friend understands and respects privacy even if you confide in them because it is still a private matter to the individual who did the confiding. Watch out for people who give their opinion and do not listen at all and do not understand. Again misery loves company. Girlfriends, girlfriends, girlfriends can become jealous of your relationship with your partner and sabotage it.

When discussing your business realize she may want what you have so be careful. It's a sad story that happens all the time. You tell her or them all the wonderful things he does and she becomes envious and before you know it she is coming over to your house when you are not home or when you are home and she starts making subtle gestures towards him. Or if you complain about the things in your relationship that should be private to him, she will either use that against you by either telling him or use it to try and get close to him and when he finds out he will feel betrayed. Everybody does not have your best interest at heart. Remember privacy is important to a man.

When you maintain a level of privacy, no one can enter into your relationship with garbage. If you look at the fraternal organization the Masons, they are the most private organization in the world. No one knows what goes on inside their house, they are a unit that is very strong.

The ideas in this book are only for a man you truly feel and know in your heart is worthy of it. "A Keeper", not an abusive man, whether it be physical or mental abuse. Abuse is abuse. Nothing in this book can help him or change him, only God can change him. This book is not to be used to manipulate a man into loving you, it will back fire. The love will not be honest or sincere. Love will never manipulate another person.

****

People are like stained-glass windows. They sparkle and shine when the sun is out, but when darkness sets in, their true beauty is revealed only if there is a light from within.

Elizabeth Kubler Ross

****

The ideas in this book are only for a man you truly feel and know in your heart is worthy of it. "A Keeper", not an abusive man, whether it be physical or mental abuse. Abuse is abuse. Nothing in this book can help him or change him, only God can change him. This book is not to be used to manipulate a man into loving you, it will back fire. The love will not be honest or sincere. Love will never manipulate another person.

If there is a dispute or if everything is good the world will never know about it. The same concept should apply to your household. Loose lips sink ships as the old adage goes.

A man needs to know he can trust his woman. Ask any man what he can't stand the most and he will tell you that he dislikes it when his woman discusses his business with her friends (meaning their relationship). Discretion is important to a man. The man in you life needs to know he can hide his heart, his dreams and his secrets with you.

The ideas in this book are only for a man you truly feel and know in your heart is worthy of it. "A Keeper", not an abusive man, whether it be physical or mental abuse. Abuse is abuse. Nothing in this book can help him or change him, only God can change him. This book is not to be used to manipulate a man into loving you, it will back fire. The love will not be honest or sincere. Love will never manipulate another person.

☆☆

Divine Love always has met and will always meet every human need.

Mary Baker Eddy

☆☆

The ideas in this book are only for a man you truly feel and know in your heart is worthy of it. "A Keeper", not an abusive man, whether it be physical or mental abuse. Abuse is abuse. Nothing in this book can help him or change him, only God can change him. This book is not to be used to manipulate a man into loving you, it will back fire. The love will not be honest or sincere. Love will never manipulate another person.

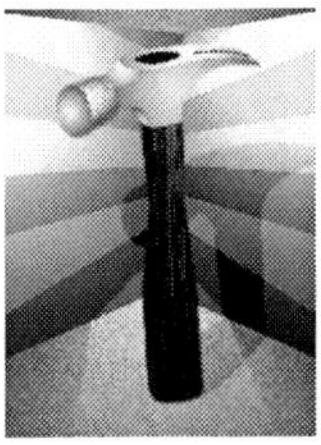

<u>*The Power of Influence*</u>

Everything in this book is about influence. As a woman do you realize how much influence you possess? My God!!! We can influence a man to do anything. Many wars have been fought over women through their influence. Yes a man will consult his advisors but ultimately he will come to his woman to discuss any major decision and then make that decision. A woman has been blessed with the power of influence. Influence is more powerful than authority. Take for example the story of Sampson and Delilah, this woman was able to convince this strong powerful man to give up the secret to his strength. She succeeded where no man would have ever succeeded. Delilah used the power of influence. A woman's influence goes way beyond Sampson and Delilah, it goes back to the mother and father of civilization, Adam & Eve. Remember it was Eve who influenced Adam to sin in the first place. We as women hold the scepter of influence for good or evil in a man's life. Adam lost a perfect existence in order to remain by Eve's side. She influenced him to defy ***<u>GOD</u>***! ***<u>WHAT POWER!</u>*** Not to say what Eve did was right but it happened and we have to recognize.

The ideas in this book are only for a man you truly feel and know in your heart is worthy of it. "A Keeper", not an abusive man, whether it be physical or mental abuse. Abuse is abuse. Nothing in this book can help him or change him, only God can change him. This book is not to be used to manipulate a man into loving you, it will back fire. The love will not be honest or sincere. Love will never manipulate another person.

Destiny is not a matter of chance; it is a matter of choice. It is not a thing to be waited for; it is a thing to be achieved.

Williams Jennings Bryan

The ideas in this book are only for a man you truly feel and know in your heart is worthy of it. "A Keeper", not an abusive man, whether it be physical or mental abuse. Abuse is abuse. Nothing in this book can help him or change him, only God can change him. This book is not to be used to manipulate a man into loving you, it will back fire. The love will not be honest or sincere. Love will never manipulate another person.

Think about all the times you have gotten your mate to do things he wouldn't have done if you didn't purr like a cat, bat your eyes or use reason. Never under estimate your power of influence. It is a function of you simply being who you are. The gift of influence is the invisible power that women overlook. The heart is the originator of all decisions. It's about getting into a man's mind.

The gift of influence is the ability to capture his mind then his heart will follow. And this is not an easy task. When you have a true understanding of the influence you posses then it will get easy. We as women lead with our hearts and this is why a man's influence in our lives is so quick and powerful. A man leads with his mind, this is why our influence over men is slow and then powerful and long lasting. Master the art of influence through his mind, soul and spirit. Ladies the physical may come first but it doesn't last. The influence of the body becomes boring to him and this is why men begin to look for spice and variety in other women. To be naturally feminine, a woman is to walk in the awareness of her importance and influence.

☆☆

A true friend is someone who is there for you when they'd rather be anywhere else.

Len Wein

☆☆

The ideas in this book are only for a man you truly feel and know in your heart is worthy of it. "A Keeper", not an abusive man, whether it be physical or mental abuse. Abuse is abuse. Nothing in this book can help him or change him, only God can change him. This book is not to be used to manipulate a man into loving you, it will back fire. The love will not be honest or sincere. Love will never manipulate another person.

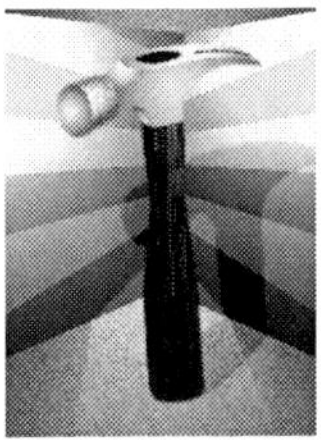

Submission

Submission, submission, oh my God what do you mean submit? I'm not submitting to any man. Let him have control over my life are you crazy! This is the response I get all the time. Don't be afraid to submit. Don't be afraid of this word. When you fully understand this whole thing about submission your relationship would be much better off. Have an open mind. Let me let you in on a little secret, when you learn to submit he will learn to submit also but when it happens to him he won't even know and now your influence becomes even greater. When you submit to your man do not do it out of obsession or obligation to try and win him or make him think you are really and truly respect his guidance and wisdom. When you obsess you leave yourself open to be abused and to be taken advantage of. The wrong man who is not worthy of submission will ultimately destroy you. You must understand the difference. When you obsess it means you will do anything and I mean anything to be with him and make him love you.

The ideas in this book are only for a man you truly feel and know in your heart is worthy of it. "A Keeper", not an abusive man, whether it be physical or mental abuse. Abuse is abuse. Nothing in this book can help him or change him, only God can change him. This book is not to be used to manipulate a man into loving you, it will back fire. The love will not be honest or sincere. Love will never manipulate another person.

★★

Life is about knowing, having to change, taking the moment and making the best of it without knowing what's going to happen next.

Gilda Radner

★★

The ideas in this book are only for a man you truly feel and know in your heart is worthy of it. "A Keeper", not an abusive man, whether it be physical or mental abuse. Abuse is abuse. Nothing in this book can help him or change him, only God can change him. This book is not to be used to manipulate a man into loving you, it will back fire. The love will not be honest or sincere. Love will never manipulate another person.

When you submit you understand his role in your life and your part to play. The man is the head of the household and in order for him to properly lead you into the right direction you must submit to his authority and direction and respect and understand the direction he is trying to lead you into. And even when you submit to the man in your life and everything in you is screaming that this direction is not the wisest choice, God will give him the grace to see his own mistakes. He will love you more because you didn't point out his mistakes and he will be more open to your counsel the next go-round. But if you point out his stupidity, his only defense is to put on the muscle and force you to do what he has asked in order to prove and secure his own position. No one should feel they have to defend their point of view to you. When you have no problem with submission he will always feel he can ask for your suggestion without judgment concerning the direction of the household. Keep in mind that it is impossible to submit when you are full of yourself. Submission calls for you to be open to direction, emptying yourself of all your own ideas on the subject to make room for other possibilities. The next step is to close the door to your house behind you. After all this submission thing is personal. It is between you, God and your partner. Submission will be easier for you if it is a private affair. Lots of time it is difficult to submit because you're too cognizant of what everyone else thinks about you submitting to your husband or partner.

Love and the human spirit are our most enduring gifts from God. The purpose of life is "growth". Soul Mates are relationships of growth. We grow to love and love to grow, thus we merge with the universal Intelligence, (GOD)! *Myrna Lou Goldbaum*

The ideas in this book are only for a man you truly feel and know in your heart is worthy of it. "A Keeper", not an abusive man, whether it be physical or mental abuse. Abuse is abuse. Nothing in this book can help him or change him, only God can change him. This book is not to be used to manipulate a man into loving you, it will back fire. The love will not be honest or sincere. Love will never manipulate another person.

Just remember all those girlfriends who think it is ridiculous for you to listen to your husband or partner go home either to empty homes or problems with their own mate.

The ideas in this book are only for a man you truly feel and know in your heart is worthy of it. "A Keeper", not an abusive man, whether it be physical or mental abuse. Abuse is abuse. Nothing in this book can help him or change him, only God can change him. This book is not to be used to manipulate a man into loving you, it will back fire. The love will not be honest or sincere. Love will never manipulate another person.

****

Love means setting aside walls and fences, unlocking doors and saying YES… one can enter paradise simply by saying YES to the moment.

Pat Rodegast

****

The ideas in this book are only for a man you truly feel and know in your heart is worthy of it. "A Keeper", not an abusive man, whether it be physical or mental abuse. Abuse is abuse. Nothing in this book can help him or change him, only God can change him. This book is not to be used to manipulate a man into loving you, it will back fire. The love will not be honest or sincere. Love will never manipulate another person.

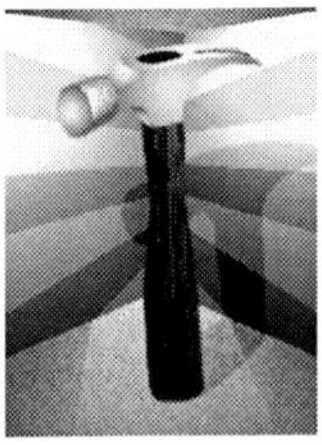

Consideration, Concern, Respect, Understanding

Boy oh boy ladies this is a real big chapter and of major concern to all the men I have spoken too. They want consideration, concern, respect and understanding the same things that we want in a relationship and most of the men I have spoken to feel that we just don't get this part at all. We as women have to prove to our "Keepers" that they are wrong, so wrong and that we do understand. You must let him do him, give him space. He needs to feel like a King. Just like you want to feel like a Queen. Respect your man as a man. So many women don't understand this, please try to understand this. He doesn't want to be treated like a child but as the man that he is. Always take his feelings and emotions into consideration. When you go shopping pick him up something nice without even asking him. Bring him home a rose and watch him beam. When he is tired and doesn't want to go to your mother's house go without him let him stay home and rest.

****

Life without love is like a tree without blossoms of fruit.

Kahlil Gilbran

****

The ideas in this book are only for a man you truly feel and know in your heart is worthy of it. "A Keeper", not an abusive man, whether it be physical or mental abuse. Abuse is abuse. Nothing in this book can help him or change him, only God can change him. This book is not to be used to manipulate a man into loving you, it will back fire. The love will not be honest or sincere. Love will never manipulate another person.

When he is watching sports don't stay in the same room and get on the telephone and talk while he is watching the game. It's about consideration for him. Consider his feelings. He will appreciate you so much more. It's about letting him be King. We want to be right all the time not realizing that we are cutting our men down. Even though you already have the answer fall back. Play your position.

Don't be judgmental about his likes and dislikes because we have likes and dislikes and that's what makes us different and who are you anyway, only God can judge him not you! Don't be judgmental about his friends – remember they are his friends – unless they are doing something illegal. If he likes to hang out with bums so be it as long as it doesn't effect your life what the hell.

Compliment your man. Just like you like compliments and praise, men like compliments and praise also. So don't be afraid to give it. When you do watch and see what happens. His chest will rise and he will beam with admiration and joy. Remember you can catch more bees with honey than with vinegar. A man likes to feel like your knight in shining armor, when you are feeling fearful let him take over and he will feel so good, my woman needs me even if you can handle it. Men are protectors and they need to be needed. Share your secrets with him.

Love may temporarily render you speechless, but when the words return they are endowed with a new beauty.

Sophia Bedford-Pierce

The ideas in this book are only for a man you truly feel and know in your heart is worthy of it. "A Keeper", not an abusive man, whether it be physical or mental abuse. Abuse is abuse. Nothing in this book can help him or change him, only God can change him. This book is not to be used to manipulate a man into loving you, it will back fire. The love will not be honest or sincere. Love will never manipulate another person.

He will feel he has access to a place in your heart that no one else has. It will make him feel like he is truly a part of you. Secrets are precious just like when he shares a secret with you it builds trust.

Share your dreams with your partner, don't leave him on the sidelines looking in like you don't need him in any aspect in helping you to achieve your dreams. Sure way to make him feel less than special. Let him help you. Let him share his dreams and you will help him achieve his goals and you will be the woman of his dreams. The key is he has to feel needed. It is responsibility.

If you do everything then he will feel like you don't need him so why am I here. Tell him what you need and allow him to answer the need. You must submit your need to him not demand your need for if you do he will surely back away and run. Find out what he needs and really and I mean really listen not just hear. And when you listen help to solve the need and that makes him feel that you care about things that are important to his heart. Remember let him know he has met your need and watch his chest get really big. A woman who makes a man feel powerful is a woman he will want to be around.

The ideas in this book are only for a man you truly feel and know in your heart is worthy of it. "A Keeper", not an abusive man, whether it be physical or mental abuse. Abuse is abuse. Nothing in this book can help him or change him, only God can change him. This book is not to be used to manipulate a man into loving you, it will back fire. The love will not be honest or sincere. Love will never manipulate another person.

☆☆

There may not be a perfect love, but love has the power to make you believe that perfection is achievable.

Sophia Bedford-Pierce

☆☆

The ideas in this book are only for a man you truly feel and know in your heart is worthy of it. "A Keeper", not an abusive man, whether it be physical or mental abuse. Abuse is abuse. Nothing in this book can help him or change him, only God can change him. This book is not to be used to manipulate a man into loving you, it will back fire. The love will not be honest or sincere. Love will never manipulate another person.

You must be creative in your relationship. Do a variety of activities to keep it alive. Everyday routine gets boring and when men get bored they start to play some place else. Stay on top of your game. Keeping your relationship alive is hard work. Are you up for it? Instead of going from home to work and back again make a date after work and enjoy each others company. Listen, no excuses, if you hold on to excuses there will always be an excuse for everything you do in life. If you don't find the time someone else will.

A man looks for a woman who can provide good solid wisdom that can lead him into the right direction when he needs guidance. Don't be a babbling idiot who preaches; lecture because he won't even consider seeking you out next time. If you don't know particular information find out and bring it back to him, then whatever you have brought to his plate let him make the choice and support him. You must be passionate about being in his corner. Being determined to accomplish the goals you have set for yourselves together.

Men want understanding. He wants to be himself. No expectations. Unrealistic expectations will also lead to disappointment and heartache.

The ideas in this book are only for a man you truly feel and know in your heart is worthy of it. "A Keeper", not an abusive man, whether it be physical or mental abuse. Abuse is abuse. Nothing in this book can help him or change him, only God can change him. This book is not to be used to manipulate a man into loving you, it will back fire. The love will not be honest or sincere. Love will never manipulate another person.

****

A first love may fill you when you are young, but the fullness of love is reached only in maturity.

Sophia Bedford-Pierce

****

Understand his point of view and I mean understand and do not patronize him, just like you don't like to be patronized. When we have a point to explain we demand they understand unconditionally, so you should understand his point in the same manner. Consider his feelings and see it from his point of view and when you do a lot of misunderstandings will be avoided in the long run.

Understand that men need at least thirty(30) minutes a day too himself when he comes home from work. When men come home they need to cool down and unwind not hear you babbling on about your day and how it went. After he has his down time then you will see that he will be more receptive too what your day was like and what is going on around the house. If you just let him take his clothes off, shower, feed him he will be ready to talk and I know this from experience.

On a spiritual basis Gods' heart seeks worship and if man was made in God's image his heart also seeks worship. Which means that sex is not a man's primary concern or objective in life. The truth of the matter is man's foremost desire is for honor, honor that comes in the form of respect and submission. All barriers come down in the face of admiration. All defenses are lowered as we enjoy our beloved and they in turn respond by drawing us closer to them. As we make men feel good about themselves, they pour more of themselves out to us.

The ideas in this book are only for a man you truly feel and know in your heart is worthy of it. "A Keeper", not an abusive man, whether it be physical or mental abuse. Abuse is abuse. Nothing in this book can help him or change him, only God can change him. This book is not to be used to manipulate a man into loving you, it will back fire. The love will not be honest or sincere. Love will never manipulate another person.

****

Do not do for the love of another what you would not do for yourself.

(Read and Re-read this one.)

Tracee

****

The ideas in this book are only for a man you truly feel and know in your heart is worthy of it. "A Keeper", not an abusive man, whether it be physical or mental abuse. Abuse is abuse. Nothing in this book can help him or change him, only God can change him. This book is not to be used to manipulate a man into loving you, it will back fire. The love will not be honest or sincere. Love will never manipulate another person.

Nothing can bring him more joy or pain than to be welcomed or spurned by the woman he cares about.

When we shower men with appreciation and words of acknowledgment, submission and honor, they strive even more to give more of themselves to us. A part of the giving honor to a man is being willing to listen to him, drawing him out and hearing his heart. It's also not criticizing when you don't understand but simply listening and praying within that God will give you the right responses if what he shares doesn't agree with you. The man in your life should feel that he could hide his heart and his dreams with you. He should feel that he could tell you anything. Believe me if he can't tell you he'll tell the secretary or some other lady friend and then that woman will have the advantage at winning his heart because she knows him.

When you praise a man it stirs up the desire within him to be the best that he can be for you. He will rise beyond the heights you've encouraged him to reach because he doesn't want to let you down. That's what you get out of praise. Learn to be his friend when he needs you. Every situation doesn't call for you to act as his partner, spouse or whatever you want to call it but be his friend. If you truly understand the true definition of being a friend and friendship then there is no need for further explanation.

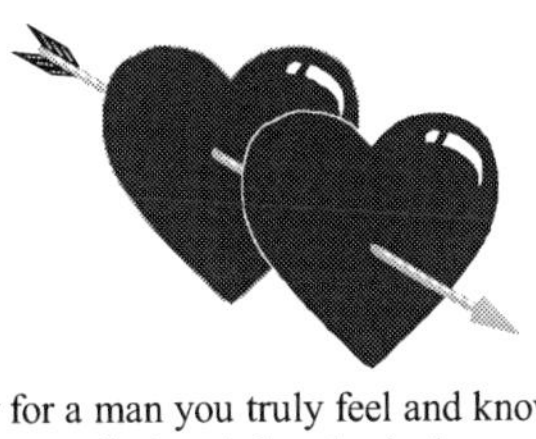

To be entrusted with another's love is the most beautiful thing in the world. This person then trusts you with all their heart.

Tracee

The ideas in this book are only for a man you truly feel and know in your heart is worthy of it. "A Keeper", not an abusive man, whether it be physical or mental abuse. Abuse is abuse. Nothing in this book can help him or change him, only God can change him. This book is not to be used to manipulate a man into loving you, it will back fire. The love will not be honest or sincere. Love will never manipulate another person.

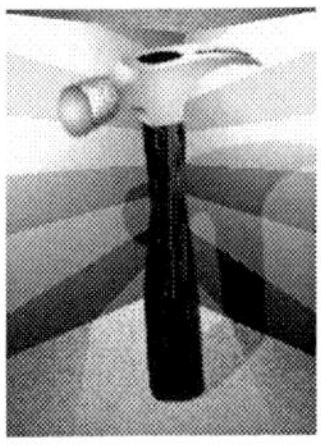

☺ Intimacy ☺

Why are so many women afraid of their sexuality? God gave it to you so express it. Men love sex! Let me repeat that men love sex! One sure way to lose him is not provide him with it. There is nothing wrong with being a freak for your spouse; he is your spouse. You should be sensual, sexy and available when he needs you. Keep saying no and trust me somebody is saying yes. I don't care how tired, angry or busy I am when he wants it he will get it. I can be angry, get some sleep or finish up what I was doing later. He can get it anytime, anywhere, anyway he wants it, end of story period! You may think I am crazy but I am not, I am just not trying to let someone else get the upper hand. What you won't do the next woman will. You may say so what, but when he does do it and you find out now you are devastated, hurt and asking why. What you did to catch that man is the same thing you will have to do to keep him. Remember what you won't do (within reason) the next woman will. So before you ask him why and what happened check yourself first.

****

The waters of life are sweeter when you drink with lips kissed by love.

Sophia Bedford-Pierce

****

The ideas in this book are only for a man you truly feel and know in your heart is worthy of it. "A Keeper", not an abusive man, whether it be physical or mental abuse. Abuse is abuse. Nothing in this book can help him or change him, only God can change him. This book is not to be used to manipulate a man into loving you, it will back fire. The love will not be honest or sincere. Love will never manipulate another person.

The notion that we can punish a man is laughable and unimaginable. A man will never do without; he will just find another source of pleasure. Don't control a man with sex, strength him with it. To create this void is to set yourself up to be replaced.

Romance what can I say. If he isn't romantic from the beginning he won't be down the road so don't expect it unless he wants it then he will give it.

Sex - Be free with your man. If you cannot be free with him then he is not the one for you. If he is going to judge you because you love anal sex for example then screw him because that is something he doesn't like and eventually you will look for someone who will satisfy that craving or any other craving you have and vice versa. If he likes oral sex hook him up because what you won't do the next woman will and do that sh_t damn good. What happens in your bedroom stays in your bedroom.

If he likes porno let him watch it and if you are not squeamish which you shouldn't be since we are all grown adults and have children, watch it with him and see what happens. There are a few things you could learn and it will spice up your love life, trust me! If he likes porno magazines let him look at them as long as the children cannot get a hold of them.

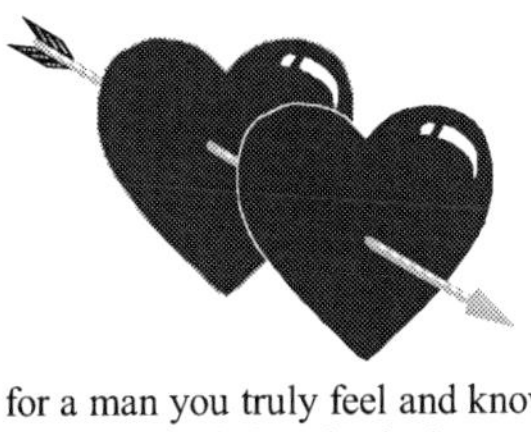

****

True love gathers strength from change within oneself and the willingness to change with one another.

Tracee

****

The ideas in this book are only for a man you truly feel and know in your heart is worthy of it. "A Keeper", not an abusive man, whether it be physical or mental abuse. Abuse is abuse. Nothing in this book can help him or change him, only God can change him. This book is not to be used to manipulate a man into loving you, it will back fire. The love will not be honest or sincere. Love will never manipulate another person.

If he doesn't have to hide what he is reading or looking at then he is more likely to open up and share with you, which is the key, the ultimate objective for him to share with you.

All men want a freak, open minded, sensual whatever you want to call it woman in the bedroom. All that not my wife, girlfriend, etc., is bullsh_t(pardon me, I'm a lady ☺). Most men wish you were a little more free and freaky. If your man loves to go to strip clubs go with him sometimes and still allow him to be himself and do not complain or criticize. Give the dollars to the women or tell him what you think is sexy. You don't have to be a lesbian to know if a woman is sexy, definitely if you are secure within yourself. I am straight and I could do a strip club or two and I think Janet Jackson is the sexiest female entertainer I have ever seen. Ask him if what he is seeing is what he likes and maybe you can give him a strip show at home and as a matter of fact you should be stripping for your man. You will both enjoy it. He can give you tips and spank you on your ass. ☺ Roll playing is wonderful thing in helping to put spice into a relationship as long as you are open minded and free.

Feel sexy, be beautiful every night when you go to bed. Give him something to look forwarded too. Men are visual. They love eye candy. Create a vision for him, a complete atmosphere of sensuality.

The ideas in this book are only for a man you truly feel and know in your heart is worthy of it. "A Keeper", not an abusive man, whether it be physical or mental abuse. Abuse is abuse. Nothing in this book can help him or change him, only God can change him. This book is not to be used to manipulate a man into loving you, it will back fire. The love will not be honest or sincere. Love will never manipulate another person.

★★

True love keeps no list of wrongs and truelove will always forgive and will continue to grow to higher levels of understanding of each other.

Tracee

★★

The ideas in this book are only for a man you truly feel and know in your heart is worthy of it. "A Keeper", not an abusive man, whether it be physical or mental abuse. Abuse is abuse. Nothing in this book can help him or change him, only God can change him. This book is not to be used to manipulate a man into loving you, it will back fire. The love will not be honest or sincere. Love will never manipulate another person.

It's about fantasy and intimacy. Be childish sometimes. Let the inner child out. Be playful not serious all the time. Sing to him even if you don't know how to sing. Be creative in creating your love nest. Spend time together without the children.

Hugs and kisses seem so small but they are big. They are valuable in emotional growth. The closeness, his soft and wet lips all together make you and him vulnerable. He begins to open up and become more receptive to you. It's about intimacy. Women we must pay attention to our men. We want attention and so do they. When he is in your presence he should be the most important thing at that time. It doesn't have to be all the time but once a week or twice a week, do cater to your man and he will forever be grateful. He wants your full attention, not competition (telephones ringing, children, work, friends) just him. Listen to him. Listen to learn and learn to listen. Give him what he wants not what you think he wants or needs.

To know your man is to reach the depths of intimacy with him. Something beautiful and special will always come out of intimate sharing. You now carry a piece of that person within you. Some secret, some feeling, some fear, whatever he felt safe enough to put into your heart and spirit.

The ideas in this book are only for a man you truly feel and know in your heart is worthy of it. "A Keeper", not an abusive man, whether it be physical or mental abuse. Abuse is abuse. Nothing in this book can help him or change him, only God can change him. This book is not to be used to manipulate a man into loving you, it will back fire. The love will not be honest or sincere. Love will never manipulate another person.

****

Love takes on many shapes but it has only one immutable rule: do not let love rule you unless you are already the master of your own mind.

(Read and Re-read this one.)

Jo Gerhman

****

The ideas in this book are only for a man you truly feel and know in your heart is worthy of it. "A Keeper", not an abusive man, whether it be physical or mental abuse. Abuse is abuse. Nothing in this book can help him or change him, only God can change him. This book is not to be used to manipulate a man into loving you, it will back fire. The love will not be honest or sincere. Love will never manipulate another person.

He trusted you not to hold his heart for ransom or exploit him by showing his jewels before the eyes of those who wouldn't recognize their value. True intimacy is built when we keep our men precious secrets they have placed in our keeping.

You share a part of each other's soul and spirit. When we know the heart of the man in our life, we will be able to stand in knowledge of his love for us. Having consideration and concern of his heart and how he thinks will give you patience and settle the temptation to personalize what might be personal issue he needs to work out on his own.
True Intimacy! ☺

The ideas in this book are only for a man you truly feel and know in your heart is worthy of it. "A Keeper", not an abusive man, whether it be physical or mental abuse. Abuse is abuse. Nothing in this book can help him or change him, only God can change him. This book is not to be used to manipulate a man into loving you, it will back fire. The love will not be honest or sincere. Love will never manipulate another person.

****

Never try to change the one you love, treasure and respect the person he or she has come to be. They will love you more for that.

Tracee

****

The ideas in this book are only for a man you truly feel and know in your heart is worthy of it. "A Keeper", not an abusive man, whether it be physical or mental abuse. Abuse is abuse. Nothing in this book can help him or change him, only God can change him. This book is not to be used to manipulate a man into loving you, it will back fire. The love will not be honest or sincere. Love will never manipulate another person.

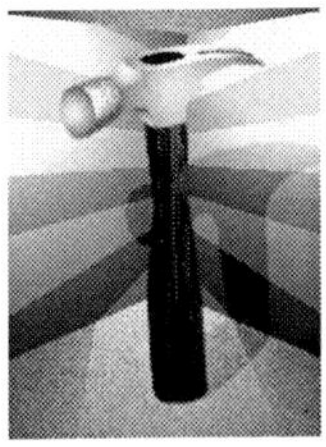

Past Relationships & Other Relationships

Once you enter into a relationship do not compare him with John whether verbally to him or mentally to yourself. He is he and John is John. When you do this you set your relationship up for failure. You cannot fully and completely love this man or experience all that love has to offer because there is a mental block for another man. Let go of the baggage. I don't care if it's Gucci. If you want to establish a new relationship with the new guy throw out the old baggage. You are not really giving him a chance to prove himself to you. The cards are stacked against him. Now that is not fair. Think if you were in his shoes and he was thinking or comparing you to Sally. Never allow another man into your bedroom. When I say this I mean mentally thinking and visualizing another man and not seeing your mate. This becomes a false affair.

The ideas in this book are only for a man you truly feel and know in your heart is worthy of it. "A Keeper", not an abusive man, whether it be physical or mental abuse. Abuse is abuse. Nothing in this book can help him or change him, only God can change him. This book is not to be used to manipulate a man into loving you, it will back fire. The love will not be honest or sincere. Love will never manipulate another person.

The key to love opens your eyes to the infinite possibilities of life, and your soul to the miracles of the infinite.

Sophia Bedford-Pierce

The ideas in this book are only for a man you truly feel and know in your heart is worthy of it. "A Keeper", not an abusive man, whether it be physical or mental abuse. Abuse is abuse. Nothing in this book can help him or change him, only God can change him. This book is not to be used to manipulate a man into loving you, it will back fire. The love will not be honest or sincere. Love will never manipulate another person.

You must first divorce yourself from your previous companion before you can really and truly invite another companion into your life. While you're in the process of divorcing yourself from a previous relationship do not compare your relationship with anybody else's relationship. What may look good on the outside maybe hellish on the inside. People have a way of putting up a farce when necessary to protect their image.

Why do woman make this mistake all the time? Compare relationships and then throw it in their man's face that John and Mary relationship is like this or that. Some women will say why can't you be more like John? He will then tell you go be with John or find someone like John. All you are doing is alienating your partner and he will get frustrated and just walk out on you because he doesn't want to hear it. Remember he maybe doing the best he can with what he has as far as money, time, patience, etc. Look at your relationship, he may be doing other things that John may not be doing for Mary. You are on the outside looking in. You know what's funny, I bet Mary wished that your partner was her partner. Think ladies before you open your mouth to complain and compare your relationship to someone else's.

The ideas in this book are only for a man you truly feel and know in your heart is worthy of it. "A Keeper", not an abusive man, whether it be physical or mental abuse. Abuse is abuse. Nothing in this book can help him or change him, only God can change him. This book is not to be used to manipulate a man into loving you, it will back fire. The love will not be honest or sincere. Love will never manipulate another person.

Falling in love may not be the answer to all of your dreams, but dreaming with love in your heart makes for a richer vision.

Sophia Bedford-Pierce

The ideas in this book are only for a man you truly feel and know in your heart is worthy of it. "A Keeper", not an abusive man, whether it be physical or mental abuse. Abuse is abuse. Nothing in this book can help him or change him, only God can change him. This book is not to be used to manipulate a man into loving you, it will back fire. The love will not be honest or sincere. Love will never manipulate another person.

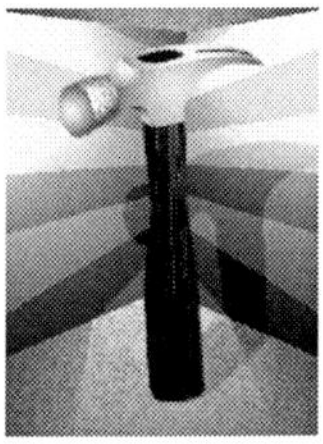

Confrontations

As the old saying goes you get more bees with honey than with vinegar. Learn to be submissive when the situation arises. Learn to hold your tongue. You know our tongues are sharp as a knife and cut very deep and leave long lasting wounds. Every battle isn't worth fighting when you are trying to win the war. For example: One Thursday night I went to particular bar and was to meet a friend of mine who never showed up but I stayed anyway, my partner knew where I was going and with whom. That was not the problem, the problem was when he found out that my friend did not show up and I still stayed at the bar and came home at 11pm. Which you might say that isn't late but for a Thursday night and I have to go to work the next day it was a problem to him. And the other problem was that for a woman his woman to be sitting at a bar by herself he felt it didn't look good. I could have said I am grown ass woman and I do what I want to do but I understood his point of view.

The ideas in this book are only for a man you truly feel and know in your heart is worthy of it. "A Keeper", not an abusive man, whether it be physical or mental abuse. Abuse is abuse. Nothing in this book can help him or change him, only God can change him. This book is not to be used to manipulate a man into loving you, it will back fire. The love will not be honest or sincere. Love will never manipulate another person.

When you are fulfilled inside, any love you have within you will shine brightly for the world to see. Nothing can dim the light of love.

Tracee

The ideas in this book are only for a man you truly feel and know in your heart is worthy of it. "A Keeper", not an abusive man, whether it be physical or mental abuse. Abuse is abuse. Nothing in this book can help him or change him, only God can change him. This book is not to be used to manipulate a man into loving you, it will back fire. The love will not be honest or sincere. Love will never manipulate another person.

Now if I had decided to fight him on this then in the long run I would lose the war because I didn't understand what he felt and respect what he felt as a man, my man. He would not trust me anymore and possibly lose respect for me. Pick and choose your battles to be fought. But remember that just because you may have won the argument doesn't mean you have won the war. You may still have a problem so make sure that the problem has been resolved or everything is in vain. Do not belittle him or be loud and disrespectful in public or private. Definitely not in public! If you want a war, you got one because now you are challenging him as a man and now he has to prove his manhood and the outcome will not be nice. If you have a problem with him discuss it, open up but in private. Two calm heads will always prevail, if you are yelling and screaming who is really listening nobody is, so it's a fruitless effort. Remember you are supposed to be the buffer in the household. You will be the music that calms the savage beast. But if he's hard headed and doesn't listen over time, he's not for you and he is not a "Keeper". Discussions / arguments are to be done in private (battles vs. wars). Your voice should sound like sweetness to his ears. Speak gently to him no matter what the subject is, even you are having a heated discussion. This takes practice. Believe me I know first hand.

☆☆

You cannot expect your love to grow and blossom if you are not willing water it and nurture it with care.

Tracee

☆☆

The ideas in this book are only for a man you truly feel and know in your heart is worthy of it. "A Keeper", not an abusive man, whether it be physical or mental abuse. Abuse is abuse. Nothing in this book can help him or change him, only God can change him. This book is not to be used to manipulate a man into loving you, it will back fire. The love will not be honest or sincere. Love will never manipulate another person.

This will make him listen and stay calm. Let your voice be music to his ears not damn it's you again what now. You can tell when he is happy to hear from you or not, it all in his voice. Just listen. Stay strong and firm during certain situations when need to be but not strong and wrong. Order is established in your home and relationship when both parties walk in agreement. A house divided, is a house that cannot and will not stand.

The ideas in this book are only for a man you truly feel and know in your heart is worthy of it. "A Keeper", not an abusive man, whether it be physical or mental abuse. Abuse is abuse. Nothing in this book can help him or change him, only God can change him. This book is not to be used to manipulate a man into loving you, it will back fire. The love will not be honest or sincere. Love will never manipulate another person.

****

If you never tell the ones that you love them, how will they ever know? The words I Love You are music to the heart and spirit that are needed on a daily basis for inner growth.

Tracee

****

The ideas in this book are only for a man you truly feel and know in your heart is worthy of it. "A Keeper", not an abusive man, whether it be physical or mental abuse. Abuse is abuse. Nothing in this book can help him or change him, only God can change him. This book is not to be used to manipulate a man into loving you, it will back fire. The love will not be honest or sincere. Love will never manipulate another person.

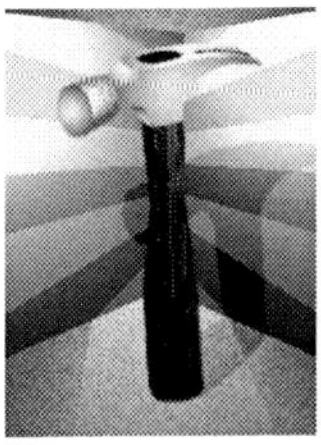

Affair Cheating

What is cheating? There are (3) three ways to cheat. First we have the obvious which is physical, doing the nasty. Second, is through the mind – your mental, when you hide your most intimate thoughts from your partner that is cheating him/her of a part of you that is so important. They are now left to figure out what is going on with you. Last but not least is emotional – when you become emotionally void towards your partner you cheat him/her from emotional growth of togetherness being a unit that is able to withstand all the outside forces that will come against you. Emotional growth is a part of our well-being. When an individual is being cheated on mentally and emotionally this is how the actual physical starts, just think about it for a moment. Think about what was going on in your relationship before you or him actually cheated. Women and men want to blame the other person without actually looking into there own relationship first.

☆☆

Love is a complex emotion that leads to an appreciation of simple pleasures in life.

Sophia Bedford-Pierce

☆☆

The ideas in this book are only for a man you truly feel and know in your heart is worthy of it. "A Keeper", not an abusive man, whether it be physical or mental abuse. Abuse is abuse. Nothing in this book can help him or change him, only God can change him. This book is not to be used to manipulate a man into loving you, it will back fire. The love will not be honest or sincere. Love will never manipulate another person.

Iyala Vanzant said something that was so profound on a radio station one day and that was " No relationship is ever destroyed from the outside but from the inside". Now really think about that statement for a minute. Something was missing or going on in the relationship. What Aretha Franklin said "You better think." Is your man going to cheat? Hell yeah! Should you worry about it? Hell no! Whatever he is going to do he is going to do. Men from the beginning of time have had multiple women, wives, whatever. This dates back before Christ. Is it right? I don't know but what I do know it's something with the male species whether human or animal. Watch the Discovery Channel or Animal Planet and you will see the lion has more than one woman, the elephant has more than one woman, tigers have more than one woman and the list goes on and on. What can be done as women? Nothing! Should a man be forced to be monogamous? Some say yes, some say no, only you can determine that for your particular situation. For me I say no. You may think I'm crazy but I am not. It's a matter of mind over matter. Men are predators and what could be done in 5 hours could be done in 5 minutes. You see it takes out the challenge of sneaking around. It's a game to them to see if they can get away with it. He may then start to think if she allows me to do this, then what is she doing?

The ideas in this book are only for a man you truly feel and know in your heart is worthy of it. "A Keeper", not an abusive man, whether it be physical or mental abuse. Abuse is abuse. Nothing in this book can help him or change him, only God can change him. This book is not to be used to manipulate a man into loving you, it will back fire. The love will not be honest or sincere. Love will never manipulate another person.

****

You can't live on love alone but it is hard to live without it.

Sophia Bedford-Pierce

****

In reading this book, yes he will love you, will he still be on the prowl, yes he will. Like I said before men are predators and they prey on the weak. Women who are the prey, smile, wink, strut their stuff in front of men inviting him in and some go for it at that moment. For most men it's hit it, quit it, and let the next man get it. It is just that they have an animalistic nature. It's a game, big hunting. We as women must learn to not open the door to invitation. Just remember he is still the man you fell in love with. Does he provide for you and your family, treat you special as the Queen in is life? If the answer is yes then what has changed? Nothing has changed just that he cheated. Don't stress out.

If you do decide to forgive him do not harp over the situation. For if you do, all it will do is make your relationship worse and very hard to deal with. If you cannot forgive him, then leave. It will eat you alive to stay. If your partner is caught cheating you have to look at yourself and see if there was something you might have done wrong in the relationship or maybe it is something lacking and whatever it maybe change it Maybe you nag him all the time, complain about every little thing or just stress him out for no apparent reason and here comes Suzy, who is willing to listen and comfort him and hear him out and now it's on.

The ideas in this book are only for a man you truly feel and know in your heart is worthy of it. "A Keeper", not an abusive man, whether it be physical or mental abuse. Abuse is abuse. Nothing in this book can help him or change him, only God can change him. This book is not to be used to manipulate a man into loving you, it will back fire. The love will not be honest or sincere. Love will never manipulate another person.

☆☆

Withhold your love and you are poorer for it; share your love and enrich the lives of yourself and your beloved.

☆☆

The ideas in this book are only for a man you truly feel and know in your heart is worthy of it. "A Keeper", not an abusive man, whether it be physical or mental abuse. Abuse is abuse. Nothing in this book can help him or change him, only God can change him. This book is not to be used to manipulate a man into loving you, it will back fire. The love will not be honest or sincere. Love will never manipulate another person.

No ladies I'm not making any excuses for men, I just want you to think and consider everything. It also goes back to the first chapter, "We are the beginning. It starts within Us." But if you feel that you didn't do anything wrong ask him why and go from there. But remember when you ask the question why be prepared for the answer. You have to ask yourself can you handle the truth.

When my partner cheated I had to learn to forgive him and deal with it, if I wanted to continue the relationship. To each his own. Remember everything isn't for everyone, it just happened to work for me. Only you know your particular situation. It didn't take away from him as a person and what he felt for me. It's about being grown and going on. Was it easy? Hell no! But I did it. His kindness, his heart, caring, understanding makes him who he is and he is still that person. He just found a prey and went for it. It's crazy, for I understand and I forgave him. Will I forgive him again, I don't know, only God knows the answer to that question.

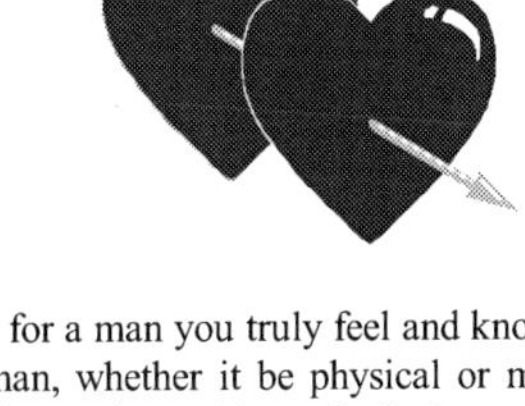

****

The key to love is to speak, and to listen!!!!

(Read and Re-read this one.)

****

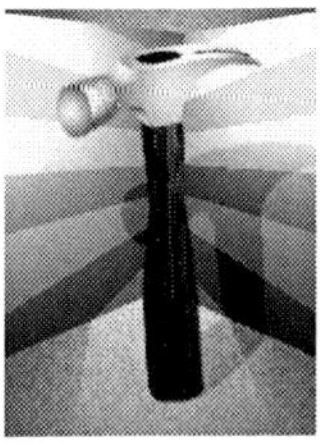

Marriage -- Partnership

Cinderella, the fairytale life that most women aspire to live. The key word is fairytale, fiction, not real. Women are so driven to be married. Well let me tell you a few things on this subject. Just because he marries you doesn't mean he not going to cheat or that he is going to be a good man. All it means is that you now have a piece of paper, changed your last name and you will get his benefits God forbid that he passes. Too many women are stressing their men out to marry them because society says this is the way it should be. Me I say screw society. Because you see when the sh_t hits the fan society isn't going to be there to help you resolve any issues you may have, so take your time. Either you are going to force him to marry you and regret it later or scare him away. Marriage is a business. It is hard work and people don't realize that until they are knee deep in sh_t and now they want a divorce instead of sticking it out and saving the relationship if it's worth saving.

At the moment you no longer hear, but only feel the music, you have succumbed, exquisitely, to love.

Sophia Bedford-Pierce

The ideas in this book are only for a man you truly feel and know in your heart is worthy of it. "A Keeper", not an abusive man, whether it be physical or mental abuse. Abuse is abuse. Nothing in this book can help him or change him, only God can change him. This book is not to be used to manipulate a man into loving you, it will back fire. The love will not be honest or sincere. Love will never manipulate another person.

We are so excited about getting married without truly understanding that as man and woman we are two different individuals trying to come together as one under one roof. We as women can keep our marriage sound and together from the beginning if we realize this fact. Remember men are not real thinkers when it comes down to this relationship thing. When I say this as I have said before they are simple, no drama, easy going concerning their relationships. Marriage should not be an underlining factor in your relationship with a man. I just want a companion/partner/friend who is there for me and I am there for him and if by chance he decides that he and I are to get married so let it be written so let it be done. I rather be treasured than be married any day. If you don't understand what I just said, then maybe you need to do some soul searching and research on the word treasured. When he treasures me it means our spirits and souls are married and no piece of paper can ever compare to that. Just something to think about. The marriage should be the icing on the cake, understand. You should want a man who will profess his love to you without thinking about marriage. When you are preoccupied with marriage you begin to lose sight of what your relationship is really about which is companionship, partnership and friendship.

Do you realize that in the eyes of God every time you lay down with a person you are married to them? Your spirits are bounded. This is why if you never sleep with your husband after the marriage you can get an annulment like it never existed. But if you sleep with him it's a lot harder now it's a divorce. It is on recorded that you consummated the marriage. So what's the purpose? A gentleman that I know asked a group of his friends why did they get married?

****

True Love, True Love, True Love can last forever and day and withstand all trials and tribulations.

Tracee

****

The ideas in this book are only for a man you truly feel and know in your heart is worthy of it. "A Keeper", not an abusive man, whether it be physical or mental abuse. Abuse is abuse. Nothing in this book can help him or change him, only God can change him. This book is not to be used to manipulate a man into loving you, it will back fire. The love will not be honest or sincere. Love will never manipulate another person.

They couldn't answer. So he answered for them. He told them that they got married because she was there for him, held him down, loyalty, children, financial, not truly being in love, not saying that they don't love their wives but the excuses were garbage as to why they got married something that will make you go hmmm. None of them said because I was in love with her, She makes me feel special, she makes me feel like a king, we laugh, I enjoy her company, etc. You know what else is crazy majority of the men I know would not get married again. If they could leave they would. So women we have to do some soul searching before we get married and find out what's really going on before we jump into something that we will regret later. Why do women feel that in order for their man to be committed to them he needs to marry them? He needs to put a ring on their finger and that makes his love legitimate. If that man is truly in love with you he will be committed to you regardless of marriage, a ring, a piece of paper, etc. It should not take that to make him love you and want to be with you and if that is the case then you need to do some self-evaluation and relationship evaluation. You maybe wasting your time in the long run and setting yourself up for failure if he feels he is forced and pressured into a relationship/marriage and you will lose. Not now but down the line you will loss. As I have stated previously I just want companionship – partnership – friendship first, if marriage happens so be it and if it never happens it won't bother me because I still have him and I am not expecting it.

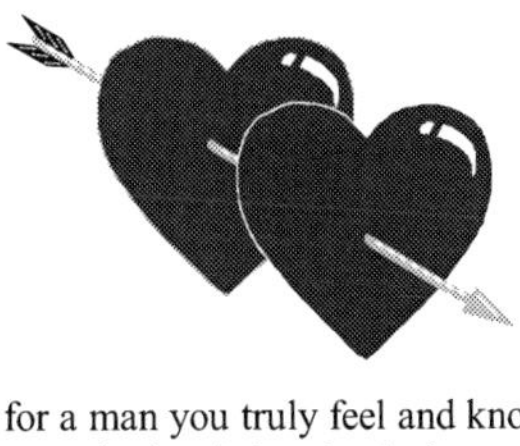

I don't care how old you are or what you have been through in life, it is never, and I mean never to late to be loved and to love.

Tracee

The ideas in this book are only for a man you truly feel and know in your heart is worthy of it. "A Keeper", not an abusive man, whether it be physical or mental abuse. Abuse is abuse. Nothing in this book can help him or change him, only God can change him. This book is not to be used to manipulate a man into loving you, it will back fire. The love will not be honest or sincere. Love will never manipulate another person.

Yes ladies, at the present time I am single and no ladies I'm not hating on women who are married or am I against marriage, just offering food for thought. I want all marriages to work out. When you take that vow it should really mean something to you within your heart and soul. When I do finally get married it will be forever and I mean forever, so that means I am taking my time on finding mister right, my mister right!

Don't get me wrong some marriages are based on love and that's a beautiful thing and God bless them and their marriages. As women we have to decide before we get married, whether or not we respect this man as a marriage partner enough to submit to him. There's that word submit again but in order for your marriage to work you have to submit and not let your pride get in the way. Pride is too expensive. It always cost us valuable relationships and wonderful opportunities. Marriage is not supposed to be a contest; it is a journey and hellava experience to be treasured.

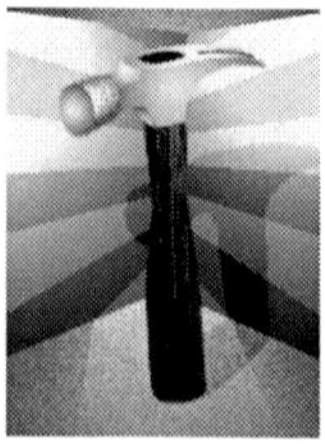

Final Thought

In loving your man remember you love him. In your life there will be certain test that will challenge your relationship and you can get pass them if you remember that you didn't fall in love with a situation, you fell in love with the person. We talk the talk so let's walk the walk. A lot of us are losing our marriages/relationships to simple things, so open up your eyes to his needs. You say you love him, he is your everything then it's time to step up to the plate and handle your business as his Queen. Anything in life that is worth having you must work very hard for it and sometimes you have to work very, very, very, hard for it. Be free if you cannot be free with the one you love then what is the purpose? Ladies let us "Maintain our Keeper". It is our responsibility to show the world that there are good men out there and that we love them very dearly and we support them to the fullest. We are their helpmeet. We are the keepers of their hearts and souls ladies.

Thank you and God Bless.

The ideas in this book are only for a man you truly feel and know in your heart is worthy of it. "A Keeper", not an abusive man, whether it be physical or mental abuse. Abuse is abuse. Nothing in this book can help him or change him, only God can change him. This book is not to be used to manipulate a man into loving you, it will back fire. The love will not be honest or sincere. Love will never manipulate another person.

Index

The ideas in this book are only for a man you truly feel and know in your heart is worthy of it. "A Keeper", not an abusive man, whether it be physical or mental abuse. Abuse is abuse. Nothing in this book can help him or change him, only God can change him. This book is not to be used to manipulate a man into loving you, it will back fire. The love will not be honest or sincere. Love will never manipulate another person.

The ideas in this book are only for a man you truly feel and know in your heart is worthy of it. "A Keeper", not an abusive man, whether it be physical or mental abuse. Abuse is abuse. Nothing in this book can help him or change him, only God can change him. This book is not to be used to manipulate a man into loving you, it will back fire. The love will not be honest or sincere. Love will never manipulate another person.

M

N

O

P

Q

R

The ideas in this book are only for a man you truly feel and know in your heart is worthy of it. "A Keeper", not an abusive man, whether it be physical or mental abuse. Abuse is abuse. Nothing in this book can help him or change him, only God can change him. This book is not to be used to manipulate a man into loving you, it will back fire. The love will not be honest or sincere. Love will never manipulate another person.

S

T

U

V

W

Y

The ideas in this book are only for a man you truly feel and know in your heart is worthy of it. "A Keeper", not an abusive man, whether it be physical or mental abuse. Abuse is abuse. Nothing in this book can help him or change him, only God can change him. This book is not to be used to manipulate a man into loving you, it will back fire. The love will not be honest or sincere. Love will never manipulate another person.

Contact Information

For information about Tracee Stukes please write to:

Tracee Stukes
C/O Chocolate Ice Publishing
2065 Fulton Street, Suite #1
Brooklyn, NY 11233
Email: chocolateice.publishing@yahoo.com
chocolateice9818@aol.com

Visit our MySpace page @
www.myspace.com/chocolate-ice-publishing or our Weblog of Expressions @ www.chocolateice.blogmaker.com, http://chocolateice-publishing.blogspot.com

All questions and comments are welcomed

For information on booking Tracee for an speaking engagement you won't forget call Chocolate Ice Enterprises
@
(347) 432-5456
Toll Free (877) Stukes1

To purchase additional copies go to:
www.chocolate-ice-publishing.com
www.booksense.com, www.amazon.com
www.barnes&nobles.com

Or call Chocolate Ice Enterprises @ the number listed above or by sending an email to the email address listed above.

Peace & Blessings

Tracee

The ideas in this book are only for a man you truly feel and know in your heart is worthy of it. "A Keeper", not an abusive man, whether it be physical or mental abuse. Abuse is abuse. Nothing in this book can help him or change him, only God can change him. This book is not to be used to manipulate a man into loving you, it will back fire. The love will not be honest or sincere. Love will never manipulate another person.

References, Resources & Must Reads

1. 101 Ways to Get and Keep His Attention
   Michelle McKinney Hammond – Harvest House Publishers

2. Conversations and experiences with men from all walks of life. (Just ask, listen and learn!!)

3. Soul Mate Connections (This is a wonderful read if you really want to know about Soul Mates.)
   Myrna Lou Goldbaum – Infinity Publishing

4. The Key to Love
   Sophia Bedford-Pierce – Peter Pauper Press

5. How to Love A Black Man (Don't let the title scare you away. All women whether Black, White, Yellow or Green can benefit from this excellent read.)
   Ronn Elmore – Warner Books

The ideas in this book are only for a man you truly feel and know in your heart is worthy of it. "A Keeper", not an abusive man, whether it be physical or mental abuse. Abuse is abuse. Nothing in this book can help him or change him, only God can change him. This book is not to be used to manipulate a man into loving you, it will back fire. The love will not be honest or sincere. Love will never manipulate another person.